Sketch

OF THE

Dabneys of Virginia,

WITH SOME OF THEIR

Family Records.

COLLECTED AND ARRANGED BY WILLIAM H. DABNEY,

OF BOSTON, DECEMBER 31, 1887.

CHICAGO:
PRESS OF S. D. CHILDS & CO.
1888.

A FACSIMILE REPRINT
PUBLISHED 1999 BY

HERITAGE BOOKS, INC.
1540E POINTER RIDGE PLACE
BOWIE, MARYLAND 20716
1-800-398-7709
WWW.HERITAGEBOOKS.COM

ISBN 0-7884-1242-6

A COMPLETE CATALOG LISTING HUNDREDS OF TITLES
ON HISTORY, GENEALOGY, AND AMERICANA
AVAILABLE FREE UPON REQUEST

CONTENTS.

Life of William H. Dabney.

WILLIAM HENRY DABNEY, the compiler of this record, was only very distantly related to the numerous Dabneys who will be found mentioned in it. He was a descendant of Robert d'Aubigné, who immigrated to Boston about the same time that his brothers, Cornelius and John, the progenitors of these Dabneys, settled in Virginia. The two branches of the family had lost all connection with each other, and it is only since the genealogical researches of William H. Dabney began, that the relationship of the Dabneys at the North with those at the South has been established beyond a doubt.

William H. Dabney was born May 25, 1817, in Fayal, one of the Azores Islands. He was the youngest child of John Bass Dabney, who was United States Consul at those islands when he was born. Mr. Dabney went to Fayal first in 1807, and finding a good business opening, solicited the Consulate as a means of introduction in an influential position, sent for his family, and soon established a flourishing commercial house. During the war of . 1812 and Mr. Jefferson's embargo, an immense business was done in those islands, simply in transferring United States products from American to British ships, and *vice versa* the products of the old world to the American vessels.

Mr. Dabney had eleven children, three or four of whom were born after his establishment in Fayal. In 1825 the little William made his first visit to the United States, in company with his father and mother and next oldest sister. The idea was to leave these children at school after a year spent in traveling about, and visiting various relatives. The trip took them as far as Winchester, Va. They spent the winter in Philadelphia, where William had scarlet fever so severely that it was not deemed advisable to leave him at school, as he was very young, and had been delicate even before this illness. He, therefore, returned to Fayal with his parents.

There was always a constant going and coming of different members of the family, who thought nothing of stepping on board of any small vessel, and starting for any point of Europe or America to which business or pleasure might call them. The family fortunes were in a flourishing condition, and Mr. John B. Dabney kept open house in the fine mansion he had built himself on a picturesque site, where he also laid out fine gardens and grounds. This place is called " Bagatelle," and is still in possession of the Dabney family. There the little boy passed two more years of happy childhood, having for playmates his niece and nephew, the children of his eldest brother, who had married in Boston, and brought his bride home to the family seat in the year following William's birth. This brother was now the head of the family, for in 1826, soon after his return from the United States, Mr. John B. Dabney died suddenly of appoplexy. His eldest son, Charles William Dabney, obtained the Consulate and continued the business. He was exceedingly well fitted in character to occupy his father's place, and was always looked upon by his younger brothers and sisters with a respect and veneration rarely to be found in the present time, even for parents.

In 1828 William was sent to Boston, without any other member of his family, in charge of Capt. Joseph Nickerson, afterwards a well-known Boston merchant. William's eldest sister, Mrs. Charles Cunningham, resided in Boston, and took charge of the little boy on his arrival. He was to have been sent to Roundhill Academy, at Northampton, Mass., but his sister finding him very small and delicate, thought a better place for him would be the family of the Rev. Samuel Ripley in Waltham. This gentleman was a son of the celebrated Dr. Ezra Ripley, of Concord, and his wife was a very remarkable woman. She had educated herself under very great difficulties in a way which few women in those days ever dreamed of. She was a fine classical and mathematical scholar, and students rusticating from Harvard, were often sent to her for care and instruction. The Ripleys did not pretend to have a regular boarding school, but took a few boys into the family, who were brought up and taught with their own children, of whom there were several. They seem to have led a very free and happy life. Waltham was then but a beautiful country village, and the Ripley boys seem to have had full run of the fine Lyman estate, the entrance to which was very near the parsonage.

Mrs. Ripley was very kind to the little boy so far from his own home, and took great pains with his education, finding him an apt and intelligent pupil. He used often to declare that he learned to look upon her as a second mother, and that the three years passed in Waltham were among the happiest of his life.

After leaving the Ripleys, William spent a year in Boston, living at his sister's, and attending the private school of Mr. Ingraham. This school was composed of thirty or more boys, among them sons of good Boston families, whose own names were subsequently honored as those of prominent citizens. It was greatly to his regret at the time, and much more so as he grew older, that at the early age of fifteen, and while very much interested in his studies, these were broken off, and the boy, for he was nothing more, was taken back to Fayal to enter the counting house, which already gave employment to three of his older brothers; a fourth, of whom he was very fond, though much his senior, had died while he was at school.

It will not be out of place here to glance at some events which were stirring up the community in Fayal, for although they were over before his return, they were still so fresh in the minds of all the family, that they remained in the mind of William H. Dabney, almost as vividly represented from hearsay, as if he had himself

partaken of the gayety and excitement. In the spring of 1832
the expedition was fitted out in the Azores to go to Lisbon, and
place Donna Maria on the throne, in place of the usurper Don
Miguel. Dom Pedro, her father, who had resigned the throne in
her favor, commanded the expedition in person, and with him
were many noted men of Portugal, besides representatives of
other nations, one of his aides being a grandson of La Fayette; and
the naval part of the expedition was in command of Admiral
Sartorius, of the British navy. The fleet fitted out in Fayal,
where there was the best port. The army collected in the larger
islands, St. Michael's and Terceira. The ex-Emperor went and
came in his little steamer, the first which had been seen in those
islands. He was greatly feted by the prominent citizens of the
place, both native and foreign. Among the many balls which
took place, one was given at " Bagatelle," where the Emperor, who
was very fond of dancing, opened the ball with Miss Emmeline
Dabney, then a great beauty. The eldest brother and his wife
were then in the United States, so that the office of host devolved
on Frederick Dabney, a young unmarried man. He was assisted
in entertaining by his sisters Emmeline and Olivia, and his cousin
Roxana Stackpole, whom he afterwards married. Mrs. Dabney,
the widowed mother, was still living, but had become somewhat
of an invalid. This was an exceedingly gay and exciting time in
the history of the little island, and the events of it made a very
deep impression on the Dabneys of that generation, most of whom
have now passed away.

In 1834 William made a flying visit to the United States, in
order to visit the dentist. After his return the Prince de Joinville
visited Fayal as a midshipman on board the corvette Syrene. C.
W. Dabney gave him a ball, and received afterwards, in return for
this attention, a tea-set of Sevres china from the Queen of France.

At this time the whaling business was in its palmiest days.
Nearly 700 vessels sailed on this business from New Bedford,
Nantucket, Falmouth, Holmes' Hole, Sag Harbor, Providence,

Newport, New London, New Haven and other ports between New York and Cape Cod. These, or those of them who made the Atlantic their cruising ground, made Fayal a regular stopping place every spring and summer, landing oil to be shipped to the United States, and supplying themselves with water and fresh provisions. This business was in the hands of the Dabneys, and gave ample occupation for all the brothers, and many clerks and employees, some Portuguese natives of the islands, others American and English. William had from a child manifested the greatest interest in shipping and all nautical affairs, and he found the intercourse with so many sea-captains and mariners of all nations and descriptions, extremely congenial to his boyish tastes. He did a good deal of sea-faring himself in these youthful days, going as supercargo in his brother's vessels.

In 1836, when about nineteen years of age, he was sent to the United States to escort his niece, Miss Clara P. Dabney, to Fayal. This young lady had been brought to America by her parents in 1832, and left in Cincinnati at the school of the Miss Beecher's. Mrs. C. W. Dabney's family had moved west to Pomeroy, Ohio, named from them, and Cincinnati; this was the reason that Miss Clara P. Dabney happened to be placed at school so far from Boston. William was to go west to get her, but met her at Philadelphia, in charge of other relatives. Nevertheless, he resolved to go on with his trip, then equal, or more than equal, to a trip to the Pacific Coast now. He went first to Winchester, Va., where he had relatives, thence by stage to Cumberland, over the National Road, thence to Wheeling, where he took boat for Cincinnati and Louisville, then back to Pomeroy and Pittsburg by boat, then staged to Erie, and took boat thence to Buffalo, visited Niagara, thence by boat to Oswego, and then by canal to Albany, where he took a steamboat again to New York; from there he returned to Philadelphia for his niece, whom he escorted to Boston, where they took passage in a vessel belonging to C. W. Dabney, and plying regularly between Boston and Fayal.

In the next year William took a trip to the West Indies with one of the employees of the house, a Mr. Cornett. The latter went as supercargo of the vessel, and William, as he said, to learn. On returning from this voyage, after being at home only nineteen days, he was sent off to the North Sea and Baltic, and this time alone as supercargo. The cargoes in both cases were of wine, in the export of which the islands at that time did a great business.

The year 1839 again saw him embarked for Hamburg, in charge of a cargo taken from a vessel condemned in Fayal, and shipped in C. W. Dabney's barque "Harbinger." After dispatching his business in Hamburg, and sending the vessel off with emigrants to the United States, he visited Bremen, Berlin, Pottsdam, Stettin, Copenhagen and Lubec, some on business, some for pleasure. He then went to London. A schooner had been chartered by C. W. Dabney to go out for fruit, oranges being then sent in great quantities from the Azores to England. She was to sail from Brixham, to which place William repaired, but finding her not yet ready, he employed the time traveling in the south of England.

The next year he visited the West Indies again, and thence went to New Orleans, from which city he made his way round to Boston, by way of the Mississippi and Ohio rivers. His sister, Olivia, was with him. The following year he went again to England, had a fearful passage, and was nearly wrecked on the Skelligs. It was the same storm in which the steamship "President" was lost. She was then the finest steamer running between England and the United States.

In 1842 another voyage took him to St. Thomas, and then to Boston. Returning from the latter place to Fayal, he had as fellow passengers, a cousin, Mrs. Parker, with two daughters, going out to make a visit. Before this visit was over William was engaged to the elder of the two girls, and two years afterwards he was married to her in Providence, R. I., at the house of her uncle and his cousin, Charles Henry Dabney. After a short wedding trip in the United States, they returned to Fayal in the autumn of 1844, Mrs. Parker and her younger daughter accompanying them. Shortly after this the American Vice-Consul in the Island of Terceira died, and it was thought a good opening for William to go and take the place, and open a business similar to that done in Fayal by his brothers and nephews. In this island, not more than fifty or sixty miles from Fayal, he and his wife remained four years, and his oldest daughter was born there. These years were very pleasant ones for the young married couple, for they found themselves received with open arms by a very agreeable and lively society, Terceira being then the military head of the Azores, and having also the Cathedral church, although the Bishop preferred to reside in St. Michael's, a larger and very beautiful island, where the main seat of government was situated. The reason for their leaving so very agreeable a residence, was the occurrence of some fearful shocks of earthquake in the year 1848. Mrs. Dabney and her mother, who was again their guest, were much frightened, and on their account Mr. Dabney hurried away to Fayal, where no shocks had been felt. His business in Terceira had never amounted to much, or doubtless they would have returned when the fear subsided, as earthquakes are by no means of frequent occurrence in the Azores.

Mr. Dabney having now no business in particular, resolved on coming to the United States, to look about him for some opening elsewhere than in the Azores. The business there was not by any means so great as it had been in the time of his boyhood and youth. There were three brothers in it, and the eldest one's sons were now grown up and in the counting house. There seemed no place for him, so in 1849 he came to the United States and spent the summer, but not hearing of anything that he liked, and the love for his island home proving too strong for him, he returned in the autumn and tried to make a new business for himself, not in opposition to his brothers, but in other lines. He took an unfinished house belonging to his sister Emmeline, and fitted it up as a residence, and there in 1850 his second daughter was born, and his only son in 1855. These were all the children he ever had, and all survive him.

In 1852, in company with his sister Olivia, Mr. Dabney made a trip to England to purchase and bring out machinery for a steam grist and saw-mill. This was quite a novelty in the little island, nothing like it ever having been set up before. A bakery was also attached to it, and Mr. Dabney even imported his baker at this time to try to introduce English bread; that made in the islands being raised with leaven instead of yeast, and being for the most part very poor. His bakery was also to make ship biscuit for the supply of whalers and other vessels. He also selected and brought out a cargo of dry-goods, the selling of which, by retail, was entrusted to a young Portuguese, a devoted friend of his.

None of these ventures proved more than moderately success-ful, and one after the other they were given up. Various experiments were tried at the mill—nail cutting, and some experiments in casting, but there was not enough sale for anything. The place was too small and too out-of-the-way, and was growing less prosperous year by year, so at last in 1860, Mr. Dabney finally did leave the home of his childhood to seek his fortune elsewhere, and he never again returned to it.

After nearly two years spent in the vicinity of Boston, looking about and meditating upon various plans, he solicited and obtained the United States Consulate at the Canary Islands. He was appointed by Mr. Lincoln, and it will be noticed that the two years spent in the United States were of a stirring kind, politically. He was here during the exciting presidential campaign when Mr. Lincoln was elected, and saw the outbreak of the civil war with all its attendant excitement. His idea in going to the Canaries was that he might there find a new field for a business with the United States. He had always disliked a cold climate, and thought that he might there make a pleasant home, similar to the one his father had been so successful in establishing in Fayal.

In March, 1862, the whole family, together with a housekeeper and a governess for the children embarked from Boston in a small vessel bound for the west coast of Africa, which Mr. Dabney had chartered to land himself and family and all their effects at Teneriffe. The passage was extremely stormy, and even dangerous. Fortunately it was a short one, and they arrived in twenty days at their new home.

Santa Cruz, the capital of the Canaries, is situated on the largest island of the group, namely Teneriffe, famed for the peak which rises some 13,000 feet from the sea. This little town of about 16,000 inhabitants, now became the home of Mr. Dabney and family for twenty years. On first arriving, he was at once visited by all the foreign residents and those of the natives, whose official or social position called upon them to come forward to receive a stranger coming as the representative of a foreign nation. He had now to meet Spaniards instead of Portuguese, and to learn the language was no great difficulty, owing to its similarity to Portuguese, which, of course, in his old home, he had learned from infancy and spoke fluently.

Santa Cruz is too warm in the summer to be an agreeable or healthy place of residence, and a more agreeable temperature is sought by the well-to-do residents, and easily found at a higher level on the mountains, the whole island being very high, without counting the peak. As the warm season was approaching, and no suitable house could be found for so large a family at a moment's notice, Mr. Dabney decided to take a house for the summer in Laguna, an old town about five miles from Santa Cruz, and two thousand feet higher. There they spent about five months, and a large house in town having been vacated in the meantime, they moved down to it in September, a terrible mistake, for this is the hottest time of all, nor is it ever comfortable till after November 1st. This year it was peculiarly unfortunate, for scarcely had they moved into the new house, when the yellow fever broke out, and they were obliged to go again into the country near Laguna. This terrible epidemic is not of common occurrence in the Canaries, but if introduced, will rage on the sea-coast, though not on the highlands and mountains. The islands have been visited some three or four times at long intervals, since they were settled by the Spaniards in the Fifteenth Century. The pest raged this time for most of the winter, but in March it was considered safe to return to town. This fever winter caused considerable embarrassment to Mr. Dabney, as he had ordered out his first cargo of American goods, and was not able to be in town on their arrival to attend to things himself. It was, in any case, an unfortunate time to start a business with the United States, vessels were hard to find, and the underwriters charged double insurance on account of war risks; the fluctuation in the value of gold, as compared with American prices, made everything very intricate and unsafe. Mr. Dabney was, however, tolerably prosperous for a time, though he met with heavy losses, and had much anxiety and worry.

Although the house he had hired was a large and very good one for that part of the world, it was on a street, in the middle of the town, and had no yard or garden attached. This was not at all to the taste of the Dabneys, who were accustomed in Fayal to own large gardens, and found a great deal of pleasure in cultivating all sorts of fruits and flowers. The climate being warm, with a little care the products of many regions and climes can be made to flourish. This was the case in Teneriffe, even more than in the Azores. Many tropical fruits, such as bananas, mangoes, dates and custard apples flourish on the coast, while from the highlands come pears, apples, cherries, and the fruits of temperate climates. Oranges, figs, apricots, peaches, plums, grapes, and many others flourish everywhere. From the time he arrived Mr. Dabney had been looking about for a house with a garden, but such were not easy to hire there, as the Spaniards prefer to huddle together on closely built streets, and do not, as a general thing, build large or comfortable houses in the suburbs. At length in 1866, Mr. Dabney hired a small house on the outskirts of the town which had a garden of about an acre and a half. He took the place on a long lease and enlarged and repaired the house at his own expense, and there the family spent the winter months for the rest of their stay on the island. The summers were spent up on the mountains, sometimes in one place, sometimes in another, latterly always in Laguna, where he had hired and fitted up another small house for the sake of its large garden. Mr. Dabney took the greatest interest in seeing as much of the island as he could, and after he became an old resident, so to speak, he took the greatest pleasure in showing strangers the remarkable and beautiful scenery of his beloved home. He made the ascent of the peak the second summer after his arrival, and afterwards at various times made many interesting excursions to different parts of Teneriffe, and to the other islands of the group, but he never left the islands to go further afield, except once in 1878, when he made a short trip to Paris through Spain, which he enjoyed very much.

As the children grew up it became necessary to send them away for their education, a terrible trial, especially to the mother, whom the enervating climate had not suited, and who became more and more of an invalid. After her return from school, the second daughter made herself useful in her father's office, but the climate did not suit her, and being full of artistic talent and ambition, she longed to be trying to do something for herself in a wider field. She left for Boston in 1872, and never returned to Teneriffe. Both girls understood by this time that their father barely made a living, and that sooner or later they must depend upon themselves. There was nothing a woman could do out there to earn anything, but one of them must of course remain at home on account of the mother, who now needed a great deal of care. After going through the Massachusetts Institute of Technicology, the son visited his home for a few months, and then he, too, went to Boston to find something to do by which he could support himself. There was no field out there.

Mr. Dabney's business had never been a stable one. There

was much competition, and being a very upright man himself, he was slow to see or suspect want of principle in others. He was often cheated and robbed by the unscrupulous, but that which finally ruined him, was the arrival of a competitor of his own nation, a sharp young man, of elastic principles. Mr. Dabney strove for some years to get along in peace with this man, but the latter never felt bound by any agreement he might make, even in writing. Mr. Dabney even had him appointed Vice Consul, hoping thus to bind him to his interests, but it only gave him more power to injure, which he unscrupulously used. At last there was necessarily an open breach, but he had by this time taken everything out of Mr. Dabney's hands except a few whalers.

The whaling business was almost extinct by that time, but a few vessels engaged in it still stopped at the Azores, as in the old times, and some of them took to stopping at Teneriffe where the water was better. From their little business Mr. Dabney derived all the income he had, for the Consulate was unsalaried, and the fees did not average $200 a year in all the time he was there. Nevertheless, there was just as much work required in reports and collections of statistics by our government, as if the place had been well paid, and there were frequently very disagreeable times as to money matters. Owing to the deplorable state of our Civil Service, many consuls think only of getting as much as possible by fair means, or otherwise, during the short time they are likely to keep their places, and, as so many of that sort are appointed to represent us abroad, the government, on principle, treats all its employés as if they were dishonest, which is very annoying to any who happen to be upright gentlemen.

In 1879 Mrs. Dabney died. The eldest daughter then became anxious to join her brother and sister in Boston, but was unwilling to leave her father alone. He was much attached to Teneriffe, and could not bear to leave, besides fearing that at his age the trying climate of New England would prove fatal to him. At last, in 1882, he yielded reluctantly to the urgent solicitations of his children to let them try to support him by their joint labor, and to make a home in Boston, where they might all be united. There he passed the last years of his life, enjoying good health, contrary to his forebodings, and remarkably active in mind and body up to the last day of his existence. He died very suddenly and peacefully, February 16, 1888.

For some years before leaving Teneriffe, Mr. Dabney had become much interested in studying up the genealogy of his family. This he continued to do after his removal to Boston, gradually extending his researches into the southern branch. The result of his labors in this direction is the present publication. This compilation gave him employment and amusement when he had left the cares of active business behind him, and was a great · resource and occupation for his many leisure hours.

O. F. D~~~

INTRODUCTION.

CHE Massachusetts branch of Dabneys, to which I belong, are descendants from Robert and Elizabeth d'Aubigné, French Huguenots, who came from England to Boston a short time previous to 1717, the earliest trace which has been found of them. They came from England whither the d'Aubigné family had fled from France, at the time of the Revocation of the Edict of Nantes, 1685, Robert being then a child. The family records state that Charles, son of Robert d'Aubigné, from whom all the Dabneys of Massachusetts and their Fayal branch have come, was born in England previous to their coming over. Another son named John, was born in Boston, but he has left no descent.

The same records state that Robert d'Aubigné changed his name to Dabney after coming to America, and that he had a brother—some say two brothers, who came over to Virginia about the same time that he came to Boston, and settled there. Hence it has always been a tradition among his descendants, that the Virginia Dabneys were descendants from the same stock as themselves, although there has never been any communication between these two branches of Dabneys until very lately, when a correspondence was commenced by the writer of this and various Dabneys in Virginia and other Southern States.

Having employed my leisure time of late years in collecting the Dabney records of the Massachusetts and Fayal branches, to which I belong, and having completed these, I felt desirous of learning something about our Virginia kinsmen, but not knowing any one of them, or their addresses, I was a long time unable to carry out my wishes. At length a friend having sent me the address of the Rev. Robert L. Dabney, then a Professor in Hampden Sidney College of Virginia, I wrote to him, asking him for information respecting the Virginia Dabneys. He promptly responded, and after giving me such information as he possessed, pointed out other Dabneys who could give me more; to these I wrote also, and they responding, gave me the addresses of others to whom I could write also. I soon became possessed of a pretty good knowledge of the Virginia branch of Dabneys, with some few of their family records. From these I wrote out a short sketch of them, and having lent this to some of those who had contributed the materials for it, for them to pass judgment on, they were so well pleased with it, that they urged me to go on and make a fuller collection of family records, with the view of having them put into print for preservation and private circulation, and having the leisure and the taste for this task, I consented to undertake it, and thus little by little I have accumulated the present collection.

I do not claim, by any means, to have collected all, or nearly all of these, but only a part of them, but I think that with this nucleus, others who may wish to follow up the task which I have commenced, may, with its assistance, complete the collection of the records of this American family, and I think that with its assistance, any Dabney may be able to trace his origin to its original source, i. e., to John or Cornelius d'Aubigné, the original settlers in Virginia.

Doubtless many errors will be found in this collection, many of which, with every care on my part, have been unavoidable, from the very method of their collection, it having been made up entirely from letters from various members of the family, scattered all over the Southern, Southwestern and Northwestern States, with whom I have no personal acquaintance. Some of these letters being obscure in their information, others very fragmentary, and others conflicting one with another, necessitating much labor to harmonize, which labor may not always have led to a correct result, still I flatter myself that they will be found in the main correct and reliable.

(*Signed*)   WILLIAM H. DABNEY.

BOSTON, Dec. 31, 1887.

NOTE.

Mr. William H. Dabney had already sent out the prospectus, and was giving his book a final revision before putting it into the hands of the printer, when his work was terminated by his sudden death Feb. 16, 1888. For a time it appeared as though his literary labor, complete as it was, yet not quite finished, would have to be abandoned. There seemed to be no one to resume it, but through the interest and assistance of Mrs. C. H. Dabney, of Philadelphia, who has sustained and carried forward the work, not only with kind and encouraging words, but also by a generous advancement of money, the book is now presented to the subscribers. The revision has been completed, but the context has been left unchanged, and the work is given to the reader just as it fell from the hands of the author, that sad, sad day in February, 1888. My thanks are also due to Miss O. Frederica Dabney, for her labor of love in preparing the sketch of her father's life, and for the beautiful likeness of him, which adorns and adds to the interest of the book.

FRANCES DABNEY.

ENGLEWOOD, ILL., Aug. 9, 1888.

Names of Dabneys who have contributed records and information, from which this sketch of the Dabneys of Virginia, and some of their records has been made.

TO THE FIRST BRANCH.

The late Rev. Edward Fontaine, the late Thomas S. Dabney, Mrs. L. Smedes, Mrs. M. S. Robinson and others.

TO THE SECOND BRANCH.

Dr. William Cecil Dabney, James Watson Woods, Rev. John Blair Dabney's Records; John Dabney, Dr. C. W. Dabney, Jr., Charles W. Dabney, Rev. Robert L. Dabney, Miss Margarett Emmilly Dabney and others.

TO THE THIRD BRANCH.

William Winston Dabney, Judge William Pope Dabney, Edwin Winston Dabney, Dr. Archie S. Dabney, Dr. William Wall Dabney, Cornelius J. M. Dabney and others.

Some few of these have contributed very largely to this book, while others have given but little beyond their own immediate record. I have therefore noted with each record the name of the person who contributed it, and thus may be seen the proportion of each contributor. I am likewise much indebted to others who did not contribute any records, but gave me much assistance in other ways. I must mention Mr. A. Dabney Barnes, of Lynchburg, Virginia, now residing in Boston.

And last, although not least, I must mention Miss Frances Dabney, of Englewood, Illinois, who has been my faithful and trusted coadjutor throughout my long investigations into this Virginia family.

To all these who are now living (for alas! two of the most valued of them have gone to their rest), I beg to tender my sincere thanks for their aid and interest in my work.

WILLIAM H. DABNEY.

BOSTON, MASS., Dec. 31, 1887.

Sketch of the Dabneys of Virginia.

ALL the foregoing named Dabneys, from whom I have heard, *with one exception*, agree in stating: That early in the Eighteenth Century, probably some time between 1715 and 1720, two Huguenot brothers, named John and Cornelius d'Aubigné, or D'Aubigny, came to Virginia from Wales, whither they had fled from France at the time of the Revocation of the Edict of Nantes, 1685.

After some years, hearing probably of the favorable settlement of the Huguenots in the lower part of the County of Powhatan, Virginia, under the auspices of King William and Mary, they left Wales and came to Virginia and settled on the Pamunky River, John on the north and Cornelius on the south side, near the Piping-Tree Ferry, where the river now divides the counties of King William and Hanover.

Another states that they originally settled on York River, and that their descendants moved up the Pamunky River, and even up to its forks, but the first statement is probably the correct one, for Mrs. Susan Smedes, in her Memorials of her father, Thomas Smith Dabney, states: "That John Dabney established himself on the lower Pamunky River, at what has been known since as Dabney's Ferry, and this became the original nest of the Dabneys of King William and Gloucester Counties."

To show the unanimity with which all the descendants of the two brothers speak of their coming to Virginia, of the time of their coming, and their supposed kinship with the New England

Dabneys, I will give the statements of several, living widely apart, and in many instances, unknown to each other.

The Rev. Robert L. Dabney, a Professor in the University of Texas at the present time, 1887, states: "The tradition which I heard from my parents was, that the stock from which we are sprung, emigrated to the banks of the York River, Virginia, from somewhere about Cambridgeshire or Norfolk, England, and that they were of the same lineage as the Daubeneys still to be heard of there. This, however, is only a tradition. The descendants moved up as far as the forks of the Pamunky River, so that the Gloucester Dabneys became so separated from the up-country Dabneys, to whom I belong, that we ceased to trace our relationship."
R. L. D.

Judge William Pope Dabney, who is a descendant of Cornelius and Sarah (Jennings) Dabney, and living at Powhatan Court House, Virginia, says: "The tradition of my paternal branch is as follows: Soon after the Revocation of the Edict of Nantes, two brothers, John and Cornelius d'Aubigné, or Daubeney, left France and settled in Wales, and after a few years came from Wales to Virginia and settled upon the Pamunky River, near the Piping-Tree Ferry, where the river now divides the Counties of Hanover and King William."
W. P. D.

Charles William Dabney, of Dalton Junction, Hanover County, Virginia, states: "The tradition of our family ancestors was to this effect, as I remember them, detailed by Dr. Shelton, a relative of the family. He represented that our ancestor, whose Christian name he did not remember, came to this country in the early years of the Eighteenth Century, bringing his family and menial servants also, and settled in what was then New Kent County, on the waters of the York and Pamunky Rivers. That the wife soon died, leaving an only son named George, and that the husband some time after, owing to the scarcity of females at that time, married his housekeeper, and left by her a numerous progeny."
C. W. D.

The late Rev. Edward Fontaine stated very nearly the same, and remarked that the Dabneys of Virginia are descended from the old Confessor d'Aubigné, meaning Theodore Agrippa d'Aubigné.   E. F.

Thomas Gregory Dabney, of Memphis, Tennessee, a descendant of John d'Aubigné, states the same, and says: "Our tradition agrees with yours as to three brothers d'Aubigné, but I was not aware that they were Huguenots, but supposed that our ancestor had gone from Normandy to England with William the Conqueror."   T. G. D.

John Dabney, of Salem, Roanoke County, Virginia, says: "Col. William Dabney was a grandson of an English farmer, who settled at an early period of our Colonial History in the County of King William, or King and Queen County, Virginia. His family were Huguenots, who spelt their names D'Aubigné, and who fled from France during the persecutions which followed the Revocation of the Edict of Nantes. Our traditions do not inform us how long the family remained in England, but the change of spelling the name to Daubeney, following the English pronunciation, and afterwards to Dabney, was adopted, I think, before coming to this country."   J. D.

His father, Mr. John Blair Dabney, in his manuscript book of family records, says: "I have never met the name of Dabney in any English book, yet I have frequently seen that of Daubeney mentioned, which I presume is a corruption of the French appellative of D'Aubigné. In the like manner, Daubeney has been transformed into Dabney. It is remarkable that there is a family of Dabneys in Massachusetts who spell their names in the same way that we do. We have no tradition or document which enables us to ascertain whether the Massachusetts Dabneys are connected with the Dabneys of Virginia, but from the coincidence in the orthography of their names, I am persuaded that they have a common origin, and that they emigrated to this country about the same period."   J. B. D.

Judge Thomas C. Dabney, of Cadiz, Kentucky, now dead, stated: "I have always understood that our family originally settled in Massachusetts and Virginia."   T. C. D.

Chiswell Dabney, of Chatham, Pittsylvania County, Virginia, says: "The tradition of our family, as far as I have been able to understand it, is that early in the settlement of America, two brothers emigrated from England to America; one settled in Massachusetts, and the other in Virginia, and I have always been taught that I had blood relations in Massachusetts, and that it was my duty to recognize them as such whenever I should meet them."
                                                      C. D.

Dr. William Wall Dabney, of Lodi, Mississippi, states: "My information, derived from the older members of my family, and also from Dr. Charles Brown, of Charlottesville, Virginia, is to the effect that every Dabney upon the American Continent are related by consanguinity."   W. W. D.

R. S. Dabney, of Hernando, Mississippi, writes: "I have learned that all the Dabneys in the United States of America are related."   R. S. D.

Again Dr. W. W. Dabney, of Lodi, Mississippi, says: "I have learned from Dr. Charles Brown, of Albemarle County, Virginia, (whose mother was a Dabney), that the Dabneys originally sprang from one of the two brothers who emigrated to Virginia when it was a British Colony, viz.: Cornelius and John, in Albemarle County, Virginia. All the records of our family Bibles were collected before the celebrated convention of the supposed heirs-at-law to the estate of William Jennings, (Interstate), of Acton Place, England."   W. W. D.

Dr. W. P. Dabney, of Powell, Arkansas, writes: "My father was descended from John Dabney, who settled in Virginia with his brother Cornelius in early Colonial history. I always understood that my ancestors were of French origin, and I think that all of the Dabneys are offshoots of the first of that name that came over."   W. P. D.

Enoch B. Dabney, of La Plata, Missouri, states: "All of the Dabneys that I have ever met with are related to me."

E. B. D.

Mrs. Susan Donaghe, of Morristown, New Jersey, who is a Dabney, states: "It is an accepted tradition in our family that the name Dabney was derived from D'Aubigné, and corrupted thus to Daubeney, Daubney, Dabney."

S. D.

Raleigh Travers Dabney, of Peoria, Illinois, says: "I have heard my father, Robert Clarence Dabney, say that his family were descendants from one of the three brothers, Robert, Cornelius or John, who fled from France during the Huguenot persecution, and settled in America."

R. T. D.

Thus from these statements of many Dabneys living widely apart, and in many instances unknown to each other, it will be seen how general is the tradition and impression among them, first as to their origin from John and Cornelius d'Aubigné; second, that these two brothers came to Virginia early in the Eighteenth Century; third, that their original name was d'Aubigné, and had been changed to Dabney; and fourth, that they and the Massachusetts branch were of the same stock, and related to each other.

Charles William Dabney, writing in reference to the tradition of the Virginia Dabneys, that they are of the same stock of Frenchmen as the Dabneys of England, says: "We claim to be of the same origin as the Daubeneys of England, who are descended from Sir William Daubigne, Knight, who came over to England with William the Conqueror, and whose name appears on the Battle Abbey Rolls, nearly at the head of the left hand column, with shield and armorial bearings quite similar to the Dabney coat of arms of the present day."

Judge William Pope Dabney, writing on the same subject, says: "On the Rolls of Battle Abbey, erected by William the Conqueror, on the ruins of the town of Hastings, where he conquered England, which I have seen, there are inscribed the names of the knights who fell, with their shields opposite to their names.

Among the Percys, the Nevilles, the DeVeres and others, appears Daubigné, with his shield."

Also among the names of the gallant squires who fell, "When groom fought like noble, squire like knight, as gallantly and well," is found the name of Daubeney. Some of the name survived the conquest. Among the names of the nobles who took care that wily King John should keep to the terms of " Magna Charter, is found the name of Daubeney."

In the novel of Marion Harland, (Mrs. Terhune), called "Judith, a Chronicle of Old Virginia," (pages 254 and 255) some of whose characters are Dabneys, old Major Dabney, pointing to his family coat of arms, tells Mr. Waring nearly the same thing, and goes on to say: " My immediate ancestors, John and Cornelius Dabnee (it is thus spelled in the old vestry book of New Kent County), fled from France to Wales after the Revocation of the Edict of Nantes, and thence emigrated to America. They were among the Huguenots who settled on the lower Pamunky River. Another more considerable body of refugees settled on the south side of James River, near the deserted capital of the Manocan tribe of Indians, now perverted into Mannakintown.

" The Colonial House of Burgesses, held at his Majesty's Royal College of William and Mary, December 5th, 1700, established the settlement as " King William's Parish," exempting said French refugees from taxation for seven years. Among these were the Michaux, still resident on the original grant; the Flournoys, Soublettes, (now Subletts); the Maurys and others."

Wm. L. Dabney, of Chicago, in a letter to Miss Frances Dabney, of same city, says: " Our family name is a contraction of d'Aubigné or Daubeney. Three of our ancestors served under King Richard the First in the Crusade, and I think that we claim relationship also with Robert d'Aubigné, who commanded a company of Swiss Gens d'armes in the time of Louis the Twelfth of France."

In Sir Walter Scott's " Tales of a Grandfather," he says: " In
1492, a body of Scotch, under the Earl of Buchan, went to
assist King Charles, of France, who was in danger of being conquered by King Henry the Fifth of England. A battle was
fought, and the Scot's turned the fortunes of the day in favor of
the French King, who, to reward the valor of the Scots, created
the Earl of Buchan Constable of France, one of the highest
offices in the Kingdom, and *Count of Aubigne.*

" In 1672 a certain French lady begged Pomponne to ask Louis
the Fourteenth to grant her permission to be naturalized an English
woman, so as to be able to profit by the presents which the King
of England might make her. The permission was granted, and
she became the Countess of Farnham, Duchess of Pendennis, and
almost immediately this last title was changed into the title of the
Duchess of Portsmouth. She received also the Ducal estate of
Aubigne in Berry, (which had been erected into a duchy in 1422,
by King Charles the Seventh, in favor of John Stuart), but
Colbert, though he made her this donation, avoided making the
Duchess of Portsmouth a French Duchess, which was her greatest
ambition. She lived during the later years of her life chiefly at
Aubigné, where she founded a Convent of Sisters."

John Dabney, of Salem, Virginia, speaking of the supposed
descent of the Dabneys from Sir William Daubenais, says: " He
was not our direct ancestor, as he was killed at the battle of Hastings,
still he may have left children in Normandy. The present accented
é of the d'Aubignés is a contraction of the old French *ais.*"

There are numerous mentions of d'Aubignés in Lingard's
" History of England," and Lord Daubeney was the Commander
of the Forces during the reign of Queen Elizabeth, and at the
time of the threatened Spanish invasion.

There are Daubeneys in England who claim to have descended
from T. Agrippa d'Aubigné, but more who date their descent
farther back to the Knight Sir Wm. Daubigné, and companions of
that time.

In collecting the accompanying records, it has become evident that the Dabneys of this country are a unique family in it, and that there are no Dabneys in it, (perhaps with only one exception, and that not really one), who cannot be traced to one of the three brothers d'Aubigné, Robert, John and Cornelius, the original settlers, for although there are some few who have not been traced back to them, as will be seen herewith, there can be but little doubt that they belong to the great Virginia family of Dabneys.

The exception mentioned above is Mrs. Sarah Osborne, *nee* Dabney, (late of Hastings, England, but now residing in Rochester, New York). She was born in Hastings, England, and emigrated to the United States only a few years since, after her marriage with Mr. Osborne. She states that she has one brother also residing in the United States, and one sister residing in England, that her father was Wm. Dabney, and her grandfather was also named Wm. Dabney, and her great grandfather was named Benjamin Dabney, and that no ancestor of his can be found. She also states that neither she nor her father ever saw or heard of any Dabney in England, or had any relatives there at all, and that her father, who died in Hastings lately at over eighty years of age, had the tradition that his family came from America, and that they had an interest in a large fortune, undistributed for want of heirs. These circumstances, together with her original ancestor, having been named Benjamin—a name so common among the Virginia Dabneys—suggest that he may have been a Virginia Dabney of the Cornelius and Sarah Jennings branch, and have gone to England for some purpose and remained there. Another fact strengthens this supposition, which is that his wife was named Jemima Gallup, and that there was a Mrs. Jemima G. Dabney died in Gloucester, Virginia, in 1821. (See *New England Palladium*, of April 3, 1821). May it not be that she, when her husband died in England, returned to the United States, leaving her son William in England?

It seems to be the fact from the statements of Mrs. Osborne, that there are no Dabneys to be found in England, and assuming that her ancestor went to England from America, and was a descendant of Cornelius Dabney, it may be that the Dabney family *i. e.*, so far as the spelling of the name is concerned, may not only be a unique family in the United States, but the only one spelling their name Dabney in the whole world.

Rev. E. Fontaine, now deceased, in a letter dated at Pontotoc, Mississippi, September 18th, 1883, says that Theodore Agrippa was the original ancestor of the brothers d'Aubigné, and "although the name has been changed from D'Aubigné to D'Aubeney, and then to Dabney, I am glad that his blood has not been much adulterated. As Episcopalians of the Evangelical-Virginia type, or as Presbyterians utterly detesting all ritualism, popery and tyranny, they are yet an educated, liberty-loving, law-abiding, progressive race. They are yet shedding the light of true religion and science, and the refinements of the highest grade of civilization wherever they go, and to give the freedom they feel to all human kind is yet their divine mission. They planned with other Huguenots the American Revolution, as the history of our family in Virginia amply proves, and with the aid of the Covenanters they fought it through successfully."

Mrs. Susan Dabney Smedes, in the life of her father Thomas Smith Dabney, entitled " Memorials of a Southern Planter," says: " The traditions among us say that we are descended from that fearless Huguenot leader T. Agrippa d'Aubigné, who flourished from 1550 to 1630. The name has undergone many changes since the American branch left France two centuries ago. It was variously written de Bony, de Beny, de Bonis, Daubenay, Daubeny, Daubeney, Dabnee, Dabney."

All agree in the statement that soon after Cornelius d'Aubigné came to Virginia, his wife, who had come with him from England, then an invalid, died, and that he soon after married Sarah Jennings, who had accompanied them to this country to assist his

wife in the cares of housekeeping. This second marriage of Cornelius d'Aubigné or Dabney, according to a statement of Charles
William Dabney, of Dalton Junction, Hanover County, Virginia,
took place in 1721. He states: " I remember seeing a Court record
in Hanover Court House (unfortunately destroyed in the Richmond conflagration of 1865.) In the first minute book of the
Court House, at the beginning of the entries, when the County
was cut off from New Kent, under date of April, 1726, was this
entry: 'Ordered that it be recorded that on this———day of
April, 1721, Cornelius Dabney, late of England, intermarried with
Sarah Jennings, also of England.'" It is founded on this fact and
date that we place the coming of the two brothers d'Aubigné to
Virginia, to have occurred sometime between 1715 and 1720, not
much before, and not later than the latter date.

Judge William Pope Dabney, of Powhatan County, Virginia,
who is himself a descendant from Cornelius d'Aubigné and Sarah
Jennings, writing about this second marriage of his ancestor, says:
"Cornelius Dabney, while in Wales, employed as a housekeeper to aid his wife, Sarah Jennings, who was a sister of Sir
Humphrey Jennings (whose estate for the want of heirs is said to
be in the Chancery Court of England undistributed); he, Jennings, was previously an obscure collier. After he came to Virginia Cornelius Dabney's wife died, leaving an only son, George,
and he then married Sarah Jennings."

Rev. R. L. Dabney relates about the same facts, and says:
" That his son, George, and family, took umbrage at his father's
second marriage, he being himself then married and having children, and separated themselves from his father and second family
of children, and moved away, and would have no communication
with them," and also states: " This history of Cornelius Dabney
is also doubtless correct and authentic in the main facts, for his
will, substantiating the same, was *extant* in the Clerk's office of
Hanover Court House, until it was burnt by Lincoln troops."

Charles William Dabney, of Dalton Junction, Hanover County, Virginia, in speaking or writing of his branch of the family, says: " Our branch of the Virginia Dabneys was the younger branch (*i. e.*, descended from George Dabney, the son of Cornelius d'Aubigné, and his first wife, who was born in England before h isparents came to Virginia), and left the family seat, where they first settled, many generations ago. Traditions and relics, as well as family histories, do not seem to have accompanied these emigrations. The lower Pamunky and York Rivers furnished their original seats, and I suspect that many traditions and records remain in the surviving family. I have known more or less intimately, at least three generations of the older members of our branch of the family, beginning with Colonel Charles Dabney, of Revolutionary fame (born probably in 1744), and I do not remember to have heard family history or genealogy referred to by any one of them. Colonel Charles Dabney, my father's uncle, who survived until December of 1829, and whom I had the pleasure of knowing intimately, in my youth, was full of character anecdotes, which he related most effectively, and in some of these his kinsmen of the older branch figured. From such sources, from old papers left by Colonel Dabney, which I have seen, and from traditions received from an early friend, descended maternally from the elder branch of Dabneys, I derive my traditionary knowledge of the family."

It will be seen that the impression is quite general among the Southern Dabneys that they are descended from T. Agrippa d'Aubigné; and that this coincides with the tradition held by the Northern Dabneys that they have descended from the same stock as Madame de Maintenon, and her brother, Count d'Aubigné, it therefore seems as if there may be some truth in this tradition. If this is true, the descent of these three brothers from T. Agrippa d'Aubigné can only be through Theodore d'Aubigné, his grandson.

T. Agrippa d'Aubigné was born in 1550, and died 1630, at the age of eighty years. He married Suzanne de Luzignon Lizee, daughter and heiress of Ambrois, Baron of Surinean, and of Renee de Vevoune. They had three children, Constant, the only son, and two daughters. Constant was married in La Rochelle, October 20th, 1608, to Anne Marchant, and their son, Theodore, was born July 25th, 1609, and he appears to have been the only child, as she died early in their married life. Several years after Constant married Jeanne de Cardillac, and they had only two children, Francoise, afterwards Madame de Maintenon, and a son, Charles, who afterwards was made Count d'Aubigné, but who never married.

We have calculated that John, Cornelius and Robert d'Aubigné must have been born between 1670 and 1676, at the latest, perhaps, two or three years before. Thus it will be seen that only one life is necessary to connect these with Theodore. May not this have been the father of these three brothers, and the son of Theodore? This has not been traced. It seems quite probable that this father's name was Charles, from the great prevalence of this name in the first generations of Dabneys in this country, there having been a continued line of Charles Dabneys through six generations in the Northern branch of Dabneys, and a continuous similar line in the second branch of Virginia Dabneys.

Theodore Agrippa d'Aubigné married again late in life, and in Geneva, Renee Burlamachi, widow of Cæsar Balbini, but they had no children.

There seems to be no doubt about the exact spot where John and Cornelius d'Aubigné first settled, i. e., on the lower Pamunky River. The foregoing statements all say this. The late Thomas S. Dabney wrote:

"That his father, Benjamin Dabney (son of George Dabney), was born at 'Dabney's Ferry,' on the east side of the Pamunky River, in King William County, and fifteen miles from Richmond, and that this was probably the place at which the original settlement was made by John and Cornelius d'Aubigné (probably by the former, as it has never changed owners), it being now in the occupancy of near relatives of his. From this spot they spread in time over the neighboring counties, and down to Gloucester, where they are now very numerous, and to other parts of Virginia, where they are not so numerous.

"From Virginia they spread into nearly, if not quite all, the Slave holding States, before the war, as they were found in North and South Carolina, Georgia, Mississippi, Louisiana, Tennessee, Kentucky, Missouri, Arkansas and Texas before the war. Since then they have spread over the Northwestern States and the Western. Some are living in California, and some few in the Northern States, such as Pennsylvania, New Jersey and New York. In Virginia they are interwoven with very many of the best families of that State, as can be seen in these records."

The late Rev. Edward Fontaine, writing of this, said:

"There is hardly an aristocratic Huguenot or Cavalier family in the old Dominion, which is not thoroughly impregnated with the prolific blood of that brave, conscientious and highly accomplished Professor of the Protestant faith (meaning T. Agrippa d'Aubigné), from whom the Dabneys of Virginia are descended. Although the name has been changed from d'Aubigné to Daubeney, and then to Dabney, I am glad that his blood has not been much adulterated. In spite of the Civil war and its ruinous effects upon the Huguenots, and in defiance of poverty and other ills, they can yet display their armorial bearings with pride."

Speaking of the chief characteristics which distinguish the Dabneys of Virginia, the Rev. J. Blair Dabney, in his book of records of his branch, says:

"In the annals of the Colonial Government the name of Dabney, as far as I can ascertain, has never been mentioned. From this omission we may presume that the Dabneys were neither politicians nor office holders before the Revolution, and probably devoted themselves to the pursuits of private industry, and the cultivation of the domestic virtues. This conjecture is confirmed by the fact that the first authentic accounts of the family exhibits

them in easy, though not in affluent circumstances, and that the
various branches of the parent stock, dispersed over Virginia, are
uniformly marked, so far as I have ever heard, by the same amiable, upright unambitious character. Though by no means grasp-
ing or mercenary, they were careful and industrious in the management of their private concerns, and were generally contented with
a moderate competency. They emerged from their privacy only
on great public occasions and exigencies when patriotism demanded
their services."

Mr. Charles W. Dabney, of Hanover, in speaking of the Dabneys, says:

"And this may introduce a remark in respect to family traits,
which latter I consider stronger evidence of family identity than
any records existing in this country, and among these traits of the
family here may be reckoned reserve and delicacy of feeling and
principle, a tendency to exclusiveness and privacy, active imagination and romantic views, all conducing to eccentricity of character,
and a marked absence of business efficiency. All the family, I
may say, have been gentlemen, scarcely one of them successful
men. Such traits as I have mentioned were out of place in such
circumstances as ours, however commendable in the abstract."

Virginius Dabney, of New York, who is a descendant of John
d'Aubigné, says:

"The Southern Dabneys have been very prolific, many as they
are, however, you will not find one of them who does not rank
socially as a gentleman. This may possibly not be entirely true of
those branches of them that emigrated to Tennessee and Kentucky,
but I believe that it may be said of them that they stand well in
their several communities."

John Dabney, of Salem, Virginia, says of these:

"I will say that they are all remarkable for intelligence and
refinement, and occupy a high, social position. Indeed, I am
proud to say that all our family, so far as I know, have been distinguished for ability, cultivation, refinement and integrity.

Although reduced since the war, their hospitality is undiminished, and they are as clanish as the Highlanders of Scotland."

It seems to have been a peculiarity among the Dabneys of Virginia, in their branches of other names, to use the name of Dabney as a prefix to their names.

Mr. Thomas S. Dabney wrote of this: " I suppose that there are a dozen or more of the leading families of Virginia that have Dabney as a prefix to their names. This is particularly notice able in the Carrs, the Maurys (witness our present Minister to Columbia, General Dabney H. Maury, and his son, Dabney), the Minors, etc., and many other examples of this will be seen in these records.

" It has been stated that all the Dabneys of the South, with the exception of one, agree in stating the foregoing origin of the Dabney family in Virginia; that exception is Mr. William Winston Dabney, of Enfield, King William County, Virginia, who has notes of other Dabneys, in Virginia, long before the supposed coming of John and Cornelius d'Aubigné, which we have placed at between 1715 and 1720, and as he supplies exact dates to these notes, there can be no doubt of their being correct." He says in his letter:

" I will begin as far back as I have any information, I find recorded in the hand book in the land office in the Capitol of Virginia."

September 27, 1664.—Cornelius de Bonis, de Boney or de Baney, a grant of land, 200 acres, in New Kent.

June 7, 1666.—A grant of 640 acres, 300 and the above 200 on Tolomoy Creek, York River.

April 25, 1701.—To Sarah Dabney 179 acres on Pamunky River, in King and Queen County.

And lands patented to James Dabney, George Dabney and William Dabney. In order to understand the situation of the lands above mentioned, I will give you the order in which the counties were formed: New Kent, from York, in 1654; King and

Queen, from New Kent, in 1691; King William, from King and Queen, in 1701, and Hanover, from New Kent, in 1720.

February 5, 1724.—Susanna Anderson's will, recorded in Hanover, leaves her son, Cornelius Dabney, all her ready money and debts in England and Virginia, and appointing her son, Cornelius Dabney, sole executor of the will. She had three children by her second marriage—one daughter, who married James Trice, and another who married Captain Thomas Carr, and one son, David Anderson.

June 8, 1725.—The will of Theodocia Jennings, recorded in the same court, leaving to her god-daughter, Sarah Dabney, some property.

February 7, 1765.—In the County Court of Hanover the will of Cornelius Dabney was recorded. He names his wife Sarah. His children, whom he names in the will, were: William, John and Cornelius; the latter died before he did, as he mentions that his portion of the estate was to be sold, and the proceeds divided among the children of his deceased son, Cornelius. He names his son-in-law C. Harris, his daughters Mary Elizabeth Maupin, Fanny Maupin and Anna Thompson, and appoints John Dabney and Henry Terrell his executors; will dated 26th of October, 1764.

Mr. Wm. Winston Dabney says: "My impression is that Cornelius Dabney married the widow Winston, as I have a copy of a deed from William Winston, in Welch, giving to Cornelius Dabney the land patented by Sarah Dabney, as son and heir of Sarah Dabney, dated in 1732.

"I read the license of Cornelius Dabney's marriage to Mary Lucy Winston, but have no copy, and think that he might have been the son of the above named Cornelius. She was left a widow, and married again a Mr. Coles. I see in the will of his son, William, that she held a dower, which she disposed of at her death. A farm which adjoins mine, belonged to George Dabney. I notice two stones, corner lines, marked G. D., 1744. I have seen a deed from James Dabney to William Dabney, stone marked 1744. This William built a brick house, and was called 'Brick House Billy,' to distinguish him from the other William Dabneys, as there were three William Dabneys just in this neighborhood. I knew two of his descendants—George, and his half brother Thomas."

The name of Cornelius de Bonis, de Bony or de Bany, which ever way it is spelled, suggests the name of d'Aubigné as the original name, and Dabney the name into which it would naturally lapse, and the name of Cornelius, so prevalent in the third branch of Virginia Dabneys, strengthens the belief that he was of the same stock or family as John and Cornelius d'Aubigné, and related to them, and the fact of his having patented lands at about the same spot in Virginia where the other two are said to have settled when they came over to Virginia, makes this still more certain; and the fact of Sarah Dabney spelling her name as such in 1701, some years before the two brothers d'Aubigné came over, as is supposed, between 1715 and 1720, shows this to have been the case.

Now it does not seem as if these two latter could have been sons of Cornelius de Bany, for he must have come over to Virginia from forty-five to fifty years before they came. Cornelius de Bany patented lands in 1664, and as a minor could not patent lands, he must have been at least twenty-one years of age at that date, which would place the date of his birth previous to 1643. If then he was not the father of John and Cornelius, what was the relationship between them?

Again it appears that Sarah Dabney patented lands on the Pamunky River in 1701, at least fifteen years before the supposed coming of John and Cornelius d'Aubigné, and that this same Sarah Dabney left these lands so patented, to her son, Cornelius Dabney in 1732. Who was this Sarah, and who this Cornelius?

Again Susanna Anderson's will, recorded February 5, 1724, leaves money in England and the same in America to her son, Cornelius Dabney. It thus appears that there were two Cornelius

Dabneys living contemporaneously in Virginia, sons of distinct mothers. How can these conflicting facts be harmonized?

In the absence of anything certain, I would suggest the following theory, which would reconcile these apparent discrepancies, and show what may have been the relationship between Cornelius de Bany and John and Cornelius d'Aubigné.

We will suppose that Cornelius de Bany was an uncle to the two brothers, a brother of their father, who escaped from France, and came as a youth to Virginia, and there settled and married Sarah ————, and that he there died previous to 1701, at about sixty years of age, and that after his death his wife, Sarah Dabney, patented other lands in 1701; that they had a son, Cornelius, to whom Sarah Dabney left these lands at her death in 1732, which date would prove that she was very much younger than her husband, or else lived to be over eighty years old.

That John and Cornelius were attracted by their cousin, Cornelius, to come over to Virginia some years after Cornelius de Bany's death; that their mother was Susanna ————, who after her husband's death in England, married a second time ———— Anderson, and moved at the time her sons came to Virginia, either with her second husband, or as a widow for the second time, and that she left money in England and property in Virginia to her son, Cornelius, who was the sole executor of her will.

The only difficulty in this theory is, that John d'Aubigné, her eldest son, is not mentioned in her will; might he not have been provided for during her lifetime, or left out for some cause, which would account for this?

That Theodocia Jennings must have been an aunt or other near relative of Sarah Jennings; she could not have been her mother, as she mentions her in her will as her god-daughter.

Respecting the patenting and deeds of lands by James Dabney, George Dabney and William Dabney, Mr. Wm. Winston Dabney gives no dates. If these were between 1701, the date of Sarah Dabney's will, and 1724, the date of Susanna Anderson's will; if near the latter date, the George Dabney might have been George, the son of Cornelius d'Aubigné by his first wife, but William and James could not have been descendants of the two brothers d'Aubigné.

If the date of the conveying of these properties was later (*i. e.*, from James Dabney to William), it may have been from James Dabney, grandson of John d'Aubigné, to his cousin, William Dabney, of Aldringham, and this William Dabney may have been the " Brick House William."

I submitted this theory to several Southern Dabneys, including Mr. John Dabney, of Salem, Virginia, Mr. Chiswell Dabney, of Chatham, Virginia, and Mr. William Winston Dabney, of Enfield, Virginia, himself, for their opinion of it. Mr. John Dabney thinks favorably of it. Mr. Chiswell Dabney, who is a lawyer, says: " I have read your paper in regard to the solution of the de Bany records, and must agree with you that it presents the only solution that is consistent with the facts, and think that you can safely proceed upon the explanation contained upon your paper."

Mr. William Winston Dabney confirms a part of it, as far as relates to Susanna Anderson having been the mother of Cornelius d'Aubigné. He writes: "I am inclined to think that Cornelius Dabney, the son of Susanna Anderson, did marry Sarah Jennings, but who his father was I do not know, nor have I any evidence of who he was."

Again, he says: " After looking over the records so much I have come to the conclusion that Cornelius, the son of Mrs. Anderson, by her first husband, did marry Sarah Jennings, who was nearly related to Theodocia Jennings. It is very plain to me, but I would have been better satisfied had I taken a copy of the records which I saw before they were destroyed."

" From Theodocia Jennings' will, I find that she mentions Sarah Dabney, Mrs. Hudson and Mrs. Blaylock, therefore I think that they were near relatives; if not daughters, they might have been sisters or nieces.

" I have Mr. Hudson's will in which he named Elizabeth Jennings, and leaves Cornelius Dabney £20 to overlook his executors.

" Theodocia Jennings had rendered in Hanover County Clerk's office her oath that she was the same Theodocia Jennings that came from England, so that I think that it may be that Mrs. Anderson's first husband may have been the first Cornelius Dabney that came to this country. (This cannot be Cornelius de Bany if his wife was Sarah.)

" In collecting these records I have failed to find any family who trace their origin to Cornelius de Bany, or to his son, Cornelius, and am inclined, therefore, to think that Cornelius never married, or if he did marry, that he left no issue; but this is only conjecture."

Respecting the Jennings' or Jennens' Inheritance, said to be still in the Chancery Court, England, undistributed for lack of heirs, Judge William Pope Dabney, of Powhatan, Virginia, says:

" Cornelius Dabney (the original settler), while in Wales, employed as a housekeeper to aid his wife, who was in ill health, Sarah Jennings, or Jennens, who was a sister of Sir Humphrey Jennings, or Jennens (then an obscure collier), and after he came to Virginia his wife died, and he married Sarah Jennings."

Charles William Dabney, senr., of Dalton Junction, Hanover County, Virginia, says:

" Several times, to my knowledge, this family delusion has broken out in its most vivid form. No doubt that the family have some tradition to guide them. The first distinct movement occurred some fifty or sixty years ago, when a regular convention of the family was held at Charlottesville, Virginia; money was contributed ($5,000, I believe), and an agent was sent to England. This epidemic recurs once in about twenty-five years, but I have not been infected with the delusion as yet."

R. S. Dabney, of Hernando, Mississippi, states: " Our branch of the Dabney family felt an interest in the Jennings' estate in England, when I was a boy, but nothing ever came of it. Then it was that the family was traced back to its origin in the United States. One Charles Brown, I recollect, used to correspond with my grandfather, John Dabney, and gave him all, or about all, the information he had about that estate. Charles Brown lived in Virginia, and was a Dabney on his mother's side."

Dr. W. W. Dabney, of Lodi, Mississippi, writes: " Thirty-five or forty years ago there was a convention held in Virginia of all the Dabney family, and all of the family Bibles collected for many generations back—in fact to almost the first settlement of Virginia, designed to prove that Cornelius Dabney, of Albemarle County, Virginia, married Sarah Jennings, who was said to be the only lawful heir of William Jennings, of Acton Place, England, who died and left an estate of £44,000,000 sterling. The Dabney family, about that time, employed a lawyer named Flourney, to go to England to prosecute their claim to the said estate. In the course of time Flourney returned, and of course accomplished nothing, but he stated that he had just got far enough with his investigations in the case to enable him to recover the estate, provided that the Dabneys would again raise about $15,000 to $20,000, as they had before done, and send him back to England, which they declined to do. I myself paid $50 towards the fund to send Flourney to England. Subsequently, and since the war, Dr. Charles Brown, of Albemarle County, Virginia (who was then ninety-three years old), went to England to look after the Jennings' estate business. Before leaving he wrote me several letters on the subject of his trip to England. I have never heard of Dr. Brown since. He was a first cousin to my father, and was a very intelligent and cultivated man; his mother was a Dabney. My old uncle, John Dabney, who was the oldest child of my grandfather, John Dabney, resided in Cornersville, Giles County, Tennessee, was very sanguine about the final recovery of the Jennings' estate, and it was in deference to his wishes that I paid the $50, to help send Flourney to England. The convention of which I made mention, as I understand it, demonstrated the fact, from the records, that every Dabney in the United States were of the same blood, and consequently all kinsfolk."

Judge Wm. Pope Dabney, in a letter dated Dec. 20, 1887, says:

" I attended a convention of the Dabney heirs at the hospitable mansion of Major John M. Waller, of Spottsylvania. (I had attended before the war a similar meeting with him in Charlottesville), to investigate our claims to the Jennings' estate. The venerable Dr. Charles Brown, of Albemarle, attended both of these conventions. We appointed at the last one Thomas Giles, Esq., who was present, and took down all the information which we could give him, and he sent them all to the Hon. Judah P. Benjamin, with whom Mr. Giles was very intimate, when Benjamin was Secretary of State of the Confederacy in Richmond. Mr. Benjamin was then, as you know, Queen's Counselor, and very intimate with Lord Beaconsfield (Disraeli), but I never heard from them, and Mr. Giles is now dead. I did not have the faith in the matter that Mr. Waller had, and his disappointment at this and his other losses caused insanity and death."

Mr. James Russell Lowell, when United States Minister at the Court of St. James, investigated this and other kindred claims, the result of which investigation may be seen in the following notice, which was published in several papers in January of 1886:

BOGUS CLAIMS.

A paper on the subject of unclaimed estates in England, prepared under the direction of Minister Lowell by Mr. Henry White, one of the American Secretaries of Legation, has been sent by the President to Congress with other State papers. " There seems to be no doubt," Mr. White says, " that many are led to believe themselves heirs to vast estates in Great Britain by designing persons on both sides of the ocean, who, with a view to personal gain, insert notices in local newspapers in the United States, to the effect that a large property left by a person of the same name of that of some well-known family of the district, or of some exceedingly common name likely to occur anywhere, such as Smith or Jones, or who distribute far and wide lists of unclaimed estates which do not exist. Large sums of money are usually thrown away by the dupes of the advertisements of fictitious lists, and a handsome revenue is made by the agents, as they call themselves, for the discovery of lost heirs, and the recovery of unclaimed estates. The *modus operandi* generally adopted by these agents is first to ask for a remittance of £2 or £3 to cover the cost of copying the Will upon which the claim purports to be based, then a large sum for the expenses of instituting inquiries, and at each successive stage more blackmail is levied, the correspondence being so cleverly conducted that several years frequently elapse before the fraud is discovered. None should contribute a dollar to unknown agents, especially toward any expense connected with establishing claims to estates in this country, until inquiry has been made of counsel here, first as to the existence of the estate, and then as to the chances of its recovery. I am told by reputable solicitors that not one claim in 1,000 of all those referred to them by the legation has any validity whatever, and very few during their long experience of claims from America have been successful."

Mr. White says the archives of the legation show that a considerable portion of its foreign correspondence is composed of letters on this subject. He describes the result of inquiries relating to the "Jannens' estate," to which there were many American claimants, showing that the property went to the heirs-at-law long before American claimants were ever heard of, and that the latter never had the shadow of title to it. Moreover, had the title once been a good one, it would long since have become worthless by the operation of the statute of limitation. "Any attempt, therefore," continues Mr. White, "to recover real estate from the Crown or individuals after a lapse of twelve years (which may be extended to thirty under certain circumstances), and personal property, after a lapse of twenty years, however valid the claim of the person making the attempt may have been originally, is certain to end in failure." All members, consequently, of the Jennens' Association of the United States of America, may rest assured that their subscriptions are simply money thrown away, if their object be the recovery of the Jennens' estate. Similar to this case are those of the " Hedges estate," the ." Bradford estate," the " Hyde estate," the " Horn estate," and many others, which are described as among the ordinary myths by which so many of our countrymen have been gulled. With regard to large sums supposed to be awaiting American claimants in the Bank of England, Mr. White quotes from a letter written by the chief accountant of that institution as follows: " There are no large amounts of unclaimed stock or dividend standing on our books. Speaking generally, without having made an exhaustive research, which would involve some considerable labor, there are very few amounts of £1,000, and probably none that exceed this sum by more than £100 or £200." And in regard to the fabulous fortunes locked up in chancery, he says: " To judge from the letters received at this legation from the United States, in reference to the unclaimed funds in chancery, many of our countrymen must imagine that institution to be a depository of incalculable millions, a goodly share of which can be easily withdrawn upon the mere institution of a claim to the same by the American Minister, and without requirement by the court of any particulars as to the name of the suit, the relationship of the claimant to the parties mentioned therein, or to original owner of the estates claimed. It is very rarely that, in any communication sent us on this subject, a smaller sum is mentioned than several millions, and frequently our correspondents state that they are entitled to twenty, fifty, and even more millions. It will doubtless cause some surprise and disappointment to such as these to be informed that the whole amount of money in the custody of the Court of Chancery at the present time is about £84,000,000, of which £83,000,000 belongs to owners who are known, leaving about £1,000,000 only of unclaimed or dormant funds."

Explanation of the Arrangement Followed in the Order of These Records.

The Dabney family of Virginia naturally fall into three groups, viz.:

First.—Being the descendants from the elder brother, John d'Aubigné.

Second.—Being the descendants from George Dabney (the Englishman, as some call him), the son of Cornelius d'Aubigné by his first wife, born in England, and a man grown when he came with his parents to Virginia.

Third.—Being the descendants of Cornelius d'Aubigné and his second wife, Sarah Jennings or Jennens.

These three divisions in this same order has been adopted, then as a matter of course, these are subdivided into generations.

It will be found that these generations follow each other in their order of ages, and that each family as it has been taken up, goes on to all its descendants, so far as I have their records, down to the seventh and eighth generations, ere going back and taking up the next one in order, which in its turn has been followed in the same manner; as a noteworthy instance, see the family of Col. William Dabney in the second branch, third generation, his youngest son Robin, and daughter Elizabeth, coming in at the very end of that branch.

First or Elder Branch

OF THE

Virginia Dabneys.

BEING THE DESCENDANTS FROM JOHN D'AUBIGNÉ

(THE ORIGINAL SETTLER.)

D

RECORD NO. I

(Given by the late Rev. Edward Fontaine.)

John d'Aubigné, the oldest of the two brothers d'Aubigné, must have been born previous to 1670, and thus have been at least sixteen to seventeen years of age at the time of the Revocation of the Edict of Nantes, in 1685. He was married in England (the name of his wife is unknown), and he must have been well advanced in years when he came over to Virginia, and his children grown, or nearly so. Only two of these are known, viz.:

SECOND GENERATION.

First.—John 2d, father of George Dabney, of Dabney's Ferry.

Second.—Elizabeth, who married Colonel William Winston, of Langaloo, and Rockcastle, Virginia.

These are the only children of whom I have any record, but there may have been others, although none have been found.

CHART OF JOHN D'AUBIGNÉ, OR DABNEY'S DESCENDANTS.

1st Generation.	*2d Generation.*	*3d Generation.*

John d'Aubigné.

John Dabney 2d.

1. John Dabney 3d.

2. Nancy Dabney.

3. George Dabney, of Dabney's Ferry.

First Wife.

4. James Dabney, The Powerful.

Second Wife.

5. Elizabeth Dabney.

6. Elizabeth Louise Winston.

Name Unknown.

Col. Wm. Winston, of Langaloo.

No. on Chart.	Index.	No. Gen.	No. Record.
	John d'Aubigné, or Dabney (original settler)	1	1
	John Dabney 2d (his son)	2	2
1	John Dabney 3d (his son)	3	3
2	Nancy Dabney, and Mr. Millar	3	4
3	George Dabney, of Dabney's Ferry, and first and second wife	3	7
4	James Dabney (supposed not to have married)		
5	Elizabeth Dabney, and William Winston, of Langaloo	2	5
6	Colonel Peter Fontaine, and Elizabeth L. Winston	3	6

RECORD NO. 2

(Furnished by the late Rev. Edward Fontaine, and corrected by Mrs. L. Smedes.)

John Dabney, second son of John d'Aubigné or Dabney, the original settler and his wife, whose name we do not know.

THIRD GENERATION.

First.—John 3d, supposed not to have married.

Second.—Nancy, who married Mr. Millar.

Third.—George, known as George Dabney, of Dabney's Ferry, married; name of wife not known.

John Dabney 2d, married a second time, the name of his second wife not known; they had one son, viz.:

Fourth.—James, surnamed The Powerful, who was so named on account of his uncommon strength.

Record No. 3 having been found erroneous, has been suppressed, and it appears pretty certain that John Dabney 3d never married, or if he did marry, that he had no children.

Mr. James Dabney, the son of John Dabney 2d, by his second wife, is supposed never to have married. He was known in his generation and since as the Powerful, owing to his uncommon strength. The late Mr. Thomas S. Dabney related the following in regard to his strength:

" My great uncle, James Dabney, was of gigantic stature and frame, and very strong. Mr. Philip Tabb, of Gloucester, of whom you may have heard, when on his way to the White Sulphur Springs, fell in with him, and they not only put up at the same inn, but were put into the same room. As they were undressing Mr. Tabb did not fail to observe that he was in the company of a man of extraordinary physical power, and his curiosity prompted him to ask my uncle to strip, as he should like to see his muscular development, and to feel of them. This he did with a laugh, and then Mr. Tabb asked him if he had ever struck a man. Yes, he replied, I struck one once, and came near being whipped for my impudence. Of course he had to tell the story.

" He had occasion to make a journey of eighty or ninety miles from home (on horseback of course), and on the way he observed a very mean looking corn field, obviously so from neglect, and seeing some negroes working on it, he inquired who was their overseer. Upon being told, he said to the negroes: 'Tell your overseer that I will return day after to-morrow, and will give him a whipping if he does not have his corn in better order.' 'Yes, Massa,' shouted the negroes, showing their teeth from ear to ear. He returned on time, and on approaching the place, he observed a man sitting on the fence, facing the road. Remembering his message, he measured the man with his eye, and saw that he was no baby. He had been observed too, and recognized as the gentleman to whom he was indebted for the message. He accordingly slipped off of the fence (the negroes coming to it at the same time) and with a bow asked my uncle if he was the gentleman who had left a message for him two days before? He acknowledged that he was, and tried to turn it off with a laugh, and as a joke, but the overseer was no joker, and told him that he had to make good his promise, taking hold of his bridle, and inviting him to dismount, which he had to do. All the rules of chivalry were observed, the horse was tied to a limb of a tree, both knights stripped to the waist and they went at it. My uncle told Mr. Tabb that he was fairly whipped twice, and on the point of giving up, but his pride came to his aid, and he held on until the overseer stopped battering him, and said he thought that they had better stop, and he acknowledged that the gentleman had redeemed his promise. The negroes in the meantime had mounted the fence, and had shouted and laughed as only negroes can laugh, throughout the fray. My uncle was laid up two weeks with his face and eyes so swollen as to make him partially blind for a week or more. He never struck another man after. I suppose that his opponent, Francisco, was the most athletic man which Virginia ever produced. He was the doorkeeper of the Virginia House of Delegates during many years, and I often saw him at his post."

RECORD NO. 4

(Given by the Rev. Edward Fontaine.)

—— Millar and Nancy Dabney, daughter of John Dabney 2d.

FOURTH GENERATION.

Dabney Millar, of Henrico, whose daughter, Nancy Dabney Millar, married Colonel Patrick Henry Fontaine, was the mother of John Dabney Fontaine, and the Rev. Edward Fontaine.

This is the only child of above known to me.

OBSERVATIONS.

Colonel Patrick Henry Fontaine's father was Colonel John Fontaine, of the Revolutionary War, who married Martha Henry, daughter of Patrick Henry, the oldest daughter.

John Fontaine was the son of Colonel Peter Fontaine, Jr., who was the son of the Rev. Peter Fontaine, Rector of Westover Parish, Charles City County, Virginia, and who was the original settler in Virginia.

Rev. Pierre or Peter Fontaine was a French Huguenot, and a son of Jacques Fontaine 2d, and grandson of Jacques Fontaine, whose life, written by himself, was so ably translated by Miss Ann Maury some years since.

RECORD NO. 5

(Given by the late Rev. Edward Fontaine.)

Colonel William Winston, of Langaloo, and Elizabeth Dabney, daughter of John d'Aubigné or Dabney.

THIRD GENERATION.

Elizabeth Louise married Colonel Peter Fontaine, Jr., son of the Rev. Pierre Fontaine, the original settler.

This is the only child mentioned by the Rev. Edward Fontaine.

OBSERVATIONS.

May not the William Winston, who married Sarah Dabney, daughter of George Dabney of the second branch of Dabneys, and grand-daughter of Cornelius Dabney and his first wife, mentioned in the John Blair records, have been the son of the above Colonel William Winston, of Langaloo? This seems to be the only way to reconcile the conflicting statements of the Rev. Edward Fontaine and the Rev. J. Blair Dabney.

Colonel William Winston's sister, Sarah Winston, married Mr. Henry, and they were the parents of the famous Patrick Henry, and Patrick Henry's daughter, Martha Henry, married Colonel John Fontaine, of Revolutionary memory. Colonel Winston was a famous hunter in his day, known as "Indian Billy," and was noted also for his eloquence.

RECORD NO. 6

(Given by the late Rev. Edward Fontaine.)

Colonel Peter Fontaine, Jr., and Elizabeth Louise Winston.

FOURTH GENERATION.

First.—John, Colonel in the Revolutionary War; died in 1791.

Second.—Mary, married first, Colonel Bowles Armistead; second, Colonel John Lewis, of Fredericksburg, Virginia.

OBSERVATIONS.

"Colonel John Fontaine," so says the Rev. Edward Fontaine, "who died in 1791, was said to have been the finest looking man in Virginia, and his sister, Mary, the most brilliant beauty of her generation. She was the ancestor of many of the Lees of Loudon; Seldens, Carys and Alexanders, of Alexandria. It is asserted that they were indebted for their beauty to their Dabney ancestry, as were the Nelsons, Moores, Carters, and other families who have an infusion of their blood."

Colonel Peter Fontaine, Jr., married Elizabeth Louise Winston, a daughter of Colonel William Winston, of Langaloo and Rock Castle, Virginia, and his wife, Elizabeth Dabney, daughter of John d'Aubigné or Dabney, the original settler in Virginia.

It will be seen that the Rev. Edward Fontaine and John Dabney Fontaine, were Dabneys through both of their parents, Colonel Patrick Henry Fontaine and Nancy Dabney Millar.

CHART OF GEORGE DABNEY'S (OF DABNEY'S FERRY) DESCENDANTS.

3rd Generation.	*4th Generation.*
George Dabney, of Dabney's Ferry.	
First Wife.	1. George Dabney.
	2. Benjamin Dabney.
	3. Dr. James Dabney.
	4. Maj. Thos. Dabney.
	Several Daughters.
Second Wife.	

No. on Chart.	Index.	No. Gen.	No. Record.
1	George Dabney.............................	4	7
2	Benjamin Dabney and Miss Armistead, and Miss Sarah Smith.......................	4	8
3	Dr. James Dabney........................	4	36
4	Major Thomas Dabney and Miss Lucy Walker, and Miss Mary E. Tompkins....	4	38

RECORD NO. 7

(Given by the late Thomas Smith Dabney and his daughter, Mrs. L. Smedes.)

George Dabney, son of John Dabney 2d, and grandson of John d'Aubigné, and his wife, whose name was Miss Smith.

FOURTH GENERATION.

First.—George.

Second.—Benjamin, who married first, Miss Armistead; second, Sarah Smith, daughter of Rev. Thomas Smith, Episcopal minister of Westmoreland County, Virginia, October 11th, 1791.

George Dabney married a second time (name unknown.) Their children were:

First.—James, afterwards known as Dr. James Dabney.

Second.—Thomas, afterwards known as Major Thomas Dabney, of Aylett's, King William County, and his residence was called the "Donnells." Married first, Lucy Walker; second, Mary Eleanor Tompkins.

And several daughters, one of whom married a Mr. Thornton, of Cumberland County, Virginia.

CHART OF BENJAMIN DABNEY'S (SON OF GEORGE DABNEY, OF DABNEY'S FERRY) DESCENDANTS.

4th Generation.	5th Generation.
Benjamin Dabney.	
	1. George Dabney.
Miss Armistead.	2. Benjamin Dabney. Ann Dabney.
	3. Thomas Smith Dabney.
	4. Augustine Dabney.
	5. Martha Dabney.
Miss Sarah Smith.	

No. on Chart.	Index.	No. Gen.	No. Record.
1	George Dabney and Susan Littlepage Quarles....................	5	9
2	Benjamin Dabney and Ann West Dabney..	5	10
3	Thomas Smith Dabney and Miss Mary A. Tyler, and Miss Sophia Hill............	5	23
4	Augustine Dabney and Elizabeth Smith....	5	29
5	Martha Dabney and Dr. Lewis Chamberlayne....................	5	35

RECORD NO. 8

(Supplied by the late Thomas Dabney.)

Benjamin Dabney, second son of George Dabney 1st, and great grandson of John d'Aubigné, and his wife, Miss Nancy Armistead.

FIFTH GENERATION.

First.—George married Susan Littlepage Quarles. He was born March 25, 1770; married December 6, 1792; died September 1, 1827.

Second.—Benjamin, who married his cousin, Ann West Dabney. (See his record, No. 10).

Third.—Ann married Major Thomas Smith, brother to her step-mother.

Benjamin Dabney married a second time Sarah Smith, a daughter of Rev. Thomas Smith, of Westmoreland County, Virginia, October 11th, 1791, then only seventeen. Their children were:

Fourth.—Thomas Smith Gregory, born at Bellevue, King and Queen County, Virginia, January 4th, 1798. Married first, Mary A. Tyler, June 6, 1820; married second, Miss Sophia Hill, a daughter of Charles Hill, of King and Queen County, Virginia; died in Baltimore, Maryland, February 28th, 1885.

Fifth.—Augustine married first, Ann Robinson; second, Elizabeth Smith.

Sixth.—Martha married Dr. Chamberlayne.

OBSERVATIONS.

Benjamin Dabney married first, Miss Nancy Armistead; she lived only a few years, and died leaving three children: George, Benjamin and Ann. A year or two after he married again Miss Sarah Smith, October, 1791. He was then only twenty-seven years old, although a widower with three children; Miss Smith was not yet seventeen. She was the daughter of the Rev. Thomas Smith, Episcopal minister of Westmoreland County (and Nomini Church, Cople Parish, from 1773 to 1776.) George Washington

was one of his parishioners. She was sister to Dr. John Augustus
Smith, President of William and Mary's College, and afterwards
President of the College of Physicians of New York. The
family seat of the Smiths was "Shooter's Hill," in Middlesex
County, Virginia; they were descended from the famous John
Smith, and have his arms—three Turks' heads. Rev. Thomas
Smith died in May, 1789, and his wife two years later, 1791, in
December, shortly after her daughter's marriage.

Benjamin Dabney had given up the family mansion at Dabney's Ferry, together with his patrimony on his father's death,
to his brother George. He made his residence at Bellevue, on
the York River, in King and Queen County; he contributed
also to the education of his half brother James Dabney, and his
wife's favorite brother, John Augustus Smith, the first in Edin-
burgh, and the last in London and Paris. He was a lawyer of
eminence, having but few peers, and no superior in Virginia. He
died in 1806, in his forty-third year, and later his widow married
Colonel Macon (James A.) of New Kent County, and moved to
his home, "Mount Prospect," in that county. Benjamin Dabney
died in middle age of pneumonia, six years subsequent to George
Washington, who died of this same disease, then but little understood.

CHART OF GEORGE DABNEY'S (SON OF BENJAMIN DABNEY, AND MISS ARMISTEAD) DESCENDANTS.

4th Generation.	*5th Generation.*
George Dabney.	
	1. Ann West Dabney.
	2. Emily Anderson Dabney.
	3. Elizabeth Camp Dabney.
	4. Susanna Quarles Dabney.
	5. George Henry Dabney.
	6. Susanna Dandridge Dabney.
	7. Mary Eleanor Dabney.
	8. Benjamin Franklin Dabney.
	9. Agnes Dandridge Dabney.
	10. Frances Anderson Dabney.
	11. Boy.
	12. James Lyons Dabney.
	13. John Fushee Dabney.
	14. Thomas Smith Dabney.
	15. Harriet Richardson Dabney.
	16. Maria Hoomes Dabney.

Susan Littlepage Quarles.

No. on Chart.	Index.	No. Gen.	No. Record.
1	Geo. Dabney and Susan Littlepage Quarles.	4	9
	Ann West Dabney (daughter of George Dabney), and Benjamin Dabney	5	10
	Wilson Cary Nelson, and Susan Dandridge Dabney, daughter of Ann West Dabney.	6	11
2	Emily Anderson Dabney and Gabriel Gray.	5	12
5	George Henry Dabney and Martha Tebbs..	5	13
7	Mary Eleanor Dabney and Benjamin Pendleton Hoomes	5	14
	Major Thomas Robinson and Mary Susan Hoomes, daughter of Mary Eleanor Hoomes	6	16
7	Mary Eleanor Boyd, nee Dabney, and Samuel H. Stout	5	15
8	Benjamin Franklin Dabney and Sarah Cary Nelson	5	17
9	Agnes Dandridge Spiller, nee Dabney, and Mr. Boughton (second husband)	5	18
10	Frances Anderson Dabney and Dr. John Taliaferro	5	19
12	James Lyons Dabney and Elizabeth Washington Dade	5	20
14	Thomas Smith Dabney and Rebecca Dylees.	5	21
16	Maria Hoomes Dabney and William N. Turner	5	22

RECORD NO. 9

(Sent by Mrs. Robinson, nee Hoomes, taken from her mother, Mary Eleanor Hoomes' Bible.)

George Dabney, the oldest son of George Dabney, of Dabney's Ferry, and his wife, Susan Littlepage Quarles.

FIFTH GENERATION.

First.—Ann West, born September 2d, 1793; married first, her cousin, Benjamin Dabney, son of Benjamin Dabney; second, married John Lumpkin, of King William County, Virginia; died 1869.

Second.—Emily Anderson, born November 22d, 1794; married Gabriel Gray, of Culpeper County, Virginia; she was his second wife, his first having been a sister of Governor Barbour, and she left four children at her death.

Third.—Elizabeth Camp, born September 27th, 1796; died unmarried, in Liberty, Missouri, May, 1866. Susanna Quarles, born as above; died in 1798. (Twin sisters).

Fourth.— George Henry, born April 8th, 1798; married Martha Tebbs, of Paradise, Essex County, Virginia (his cousin on mother's side); died May 27th, 1842.

Fifth.—Susanna Dandridge, born November 26th, 1799; died in 1800.

Sixth.—Mary Eleanor, born February 7th, 1801; married at fifteen Benjamin Pendleton Hoomes, November 21, 1816.

Seventh.—Benjamin Franklin, born October 12th, 1802; married Miss Nelson, a daughter of Thomas Cary Nelson, of King William County, Virginia; died.

Eighth.—Agnes Dandridge, born June 29th, 1804; married first, Dr. George Augustus Spiller; second, Mr. Boughton; died June 13th, 1880.

Ninth.—Frances Anderson, born January 31st, 1806; married first, Dr. John Taliaferro; married second, Custis Carter; died.

Tenth.—A boy, born and died April 23d, 1807.

Eleventh.—James Lyons, born July 25th, 1808; married Elizabeth Washington Dade, daughter of Major Dade, of Fauquier County, Virginia; died.

Twelfth.—John Fushee, born December 10th, 1810; died in 1811.

Thirteenth.—Thomas Smith, born April 7th, 1812; married Rebecca Dylees; living in 1883 in Liberty County, Missouri.

Fourteenth.—Harriet Richardson, born September 12th, 1815; died in 1817.

Fifteenth.—Maria Hoomes, born December 2d, 1817; married William F. Turner, her cousin; died.

Sixteen children, all noted for beauty.

Mrs. George Dabney was married at fourteen years of age, and died April 16th, 1827, aged forty-nine years. She was born March 12th, 1778.

Mr. George Dabney's place was called "Greenville." It is near the Pamunky River, which divides King William from Hanover County. Dabney's Ferry crosses the river just there, and so he

has always been known as " George Dabney, of Dabney's Ferry,"
to distinguish him from other George Dabneys.

Hanover Town was on the height just over the river. It was
a large village before the war, but now has not a house standing.

George Dabney was celebrated in his youth for his great
strength, and indeed throughout his whole life, and he became
famous for this at William and Mary's College, as did also his
brother, Benjamin, although in a less degree. In this they
resembled their grandfather's half brother, James Dabney, who
bears the surname of " The Powerful " on the Family Tree. He
entered the United States Navy, and was present at the Battle of
Tripoli, where he had the good fortune to save the life of Decatur,
by transfixing his assailant (who was about to kill him, and who
was a gigantic pirate) with his bayonet, and throwing him into
the sea. He, however, soon grew tired of the navy, and left it
for a planter's life.

Mr. George Dabney, as has been stated, was of great stature
and strength. The late Thomas S. Dabney gives the following
anecdote in regard to his strength:

" My half brother George was a very strong man; he once
killed a large dog with his fist at a single blow, and may have
killed a man in this city (Baltimore) in the same way, but this is
not certainly known. He had come here with his wheat and sold
it, and imprudently drawn the money, and more imprudently still,
had gone out on a spree after dark, and had pulled out his money
in a drinking establishment to pay for some drinks. This was
noticed by a ruffian, who followed him, and attempted to stab him
from behind, but the dirk struck the knife that was in his pocket,
splitting the buckhorn casing, and only giving my brother a jar.
He threw his left hand round behind, seized the fellow by the
collar and felled him to the pavement, and he appeared to be dead.
He had but one of two things to do, to call the watch, or to escape
to his schooner, which was to sail in the morning. He called the
watch; he showed them the broken pointed dirk which lay on the

pavement, his broken knife, the pocket of his waistcoat, and the gash that had been made in his waistcoat by the dirk. The watchman believed my brother's account of the affair and did not arrest him, but summoned him to attend at the Police Court on the following morning, but he was far down the bay by that hour, and heard no more about the ruffian. This unusual physical development must have been due to his mother's family (she was an Armistead) as none of the children of the second marriage were remarkable for their prowess."

RECORD NO. 10

(Given by Mrs. Robinson.)

Benjamin Dabney, second son of Benjamin Dabney and Miss Armistead, and his cousin, Ann West Dabney, the oldest child of George Dabney, of Dabney's Ferry, and Susan Littlepage Quarles. They had several children, of which only three lived to grow up.

SIXTH GENERATION.

First.—Susan Dandridge married Wilson Cary Nelson, brother of the wife of Benjamin Franklin Dabney, her uncle.

Second.—Mary Booth married Mr. Bosher, and lives in Richmond.

Third.—Thomas Jefferson, born previous to 1826; married Miss Mary Wright, of Essex County, Virginia; they had one daughter who died in childhood. He is living at date (1886).

OBSERVATIONS.

Benjamin Dabney was a very handsome and strong young man, and was the champion of the college, when at William and Mary's College, but he was not so strong as his brother George, who was celebrated for his great strength. They both inherited their great strength from their mother's ancestors, the Armisteads.

Mrs. Dabney was named for Benjamin West, the great painter, who was a near relative of her mother's. She married a second time John Lumpkin, of Dover, King William County, Virginia, and had a daughter named:

Fourth.—Laura, who married Lucius Harrison; he died, leaving her with one son and four daughters; son and oldest daughter married. She lives in Richmond.

Wilson Cary Nelson and Susan Dandridge Dabney, daughter of Benjamin and Ann West Dabney.

SEVENTH GENERATION.

First.—Benjamin Cary married Miss Betty Martin, and has many children.

Second.—Sarah Day married Dr. Thomas Gregory, of King William County, Virginia. He was a relative of his wife; she died young, leaving one daughter, Kate, who married John Watkins Dabney.

Third.—Nannie married O. M. Winston, Clerk of King William County, Virginia; has two daughters, one named Nannie, who married Augustus Hill, and has four daughters (1886).

Fourth.—Mary Winston married Moore Brockenbrough Wright, a merchant of Tappahannock.

Fifth.—Maria Russell Jones married first (name unknown); he died during the Civil War, and his widow married again a Mr. Waring.

Sixth.—A daughter (name unknown), who married John Jones, of Texas.

OBSERVATIONS.

Mr. W. C. Nelson was brother to Sallie Cary Nelson, who married Benjamin Franklin Dabney, son of George and Susan Quarles Dabney. Kate Gregory, daughter of Sarah Day Nelson and Dr. Thomas Gregory, married John Watkins Dabney, a son of Charles W. Dabney, of Dalton Junction, Hanover County, Virginia, and is now living (1887) in Jundiahi, Sao Pauli, Brazil, as a missionary. They have a family of children.

RECORD NO. 12
(Given by Mrs. Robinson.)

Gabriel Gray and Emily Anderson Dabney, second child of George Dabney and Susan L. Quarles.

SIXTH GENERATION.

First.—George Dabney, a lawyer, lives at Culpeper Court House; married a Miss Johnson, of Charlotte, and has two daughters (one married).

Second.—Gabriel, a graduate of V. M. Institute, is married, and has one son.

Third.—Thomas left home very young, and nothing is known about him.

Fourth.—Susan Dabney married her father's nephew, Mr. Gibson, who died and left her with one son and one daughter. Mrs. Gibson married again Mr. Ashbrook, of Paris, Kentucky, where they now live and have several children. Her daughter, by her first husband, is married, and has several children.

Fifth.—Mary married her cousin on her father's side, Mr. Walker. They live in Madison County, and have several children.

OBSERVATIONS.

Mr. Gabriel Gay, Sr., is a Baptist minister in Fincastle, Roanoke County, Virginia. He was twice married; his first wife having been a sister of Governor Barbour, of Virginia. She left four children at her death.

RECORD NO. 13
(Supplied by Mrs. Robinson.)

George Henry Dabney, oldest son, and the fourth child of George Dabney and Susan L. Quarles, and his wife, Martha Tebbs.

SIXTH GENERATION.

First.—Thomas married a widow with a grown up daughter. They have no children; they moved South, and he was still living in 1881.

Second.—Nannie, married, and living at Bethany, Brook County, Virginia, and has children.

OBSERVATIONS.

Mrs. Dabney was own cousin to her husband. Her father's place, " Paradise," is on the banks of the Rappahanock River.

RECORD NO. 14
(Supplied by Mrs. Robinson.)

Benjamin Pendleton Hoomes and Mary Eleanor Dabney, seventh child of George Dabney and Susan L. Quarles.

SIXTH GENERATION.

First.—Mary Susan, born August 19th, 1817; married Major, Thomas Robinson, son of Major Beverly Robinson and Sarah Cose Downing, of Northumberland, Virginia. Living at date at Aylett's, King William County, Virginia. They were married May 11th, 1835.

Second.—George Dabney, born in 1818; died in 1822.

Third.—Thomas Clairborne, born in 1820; died in 1822.

Fourth.—Benjamin Pendleton, Jr., born in 1821, three month's after his father's death; married a Kentucky lady, and lives in Kentucky; has three sons and one daughter living in Cincinnati.

OBSERVATIONS.

Mr. Hoomes (pronounced Homes) was a son of a British officer, who fought on the American side in the war of the Revolution. He died five years after marriage, August 16th, 1821, leaving his widow, then only twenty years of age, with one daughter; a son was born three months after his father's death. Mrs. Hoomes was very beautiful. In 1825 she married again Colonel William Boyd, of Clifton, King and Queen County, Virginia. He died very suddenly three weeks after their marriage.

RECORD NO. 15
(Supplied by Mrs. Robinson.)

In 1828 Mrs. Boyd, *nee* Dabney, married a third time Samuel H. Stout, of Orange Court House, and went there to reside. Their children were:

SIXTH GENERATION.

First.—Samuel, married, and living in Covington, Kentucky, and has children.

Second.—Thomas Henry, who is a Baptist minister in Eufaula, Alabama. He has a son by his first wife, named Thomas, who is married, and lives in Texas.

Third.—John Lumpkin, who is a lawyer, and lives in Bowling Green, Kentucky, is married, and has children.

Fourth.—Emily married Lewis Henry Garnett, son of Judge Garnett, of Essex County, Virginia; she died young, leaving one son, Carroll Garnett, of Front Royal, Warren County, Virginia.

Fifth.—Robert.

OBSERVATIONS.

Mrs. Stout, in her youth, was very beautiful, as were her sisters, and she attracted thereby the attention of General Lafayette when he visited Richmond in 1825.

RECORD NO. 16

(Supplied by Mrs. Robinson.)

Major Thomas Robinson and Mary Susan Hoomes, only daughter of Benjamin Pendleton Hoomes and Mary Eleanor Dabney.

SEVENTH GENERATION.

First.—Beverly married Fanny Hill, and lives in Lancaster County, Virginia; has one son, Beverly, Jr., and two daughters.

Second.—Mary Eleanor married first, Westmore Waring, who died, leaving her with three sons; married a second time the brother of her first husband, Spencer Roane Waring, and has one daughter.

Third.—Benjamin Hoomes married Emily Reynolds Whitelaw, and has a son and daughter.

Fourth.—Eugene Downing married Adelaide Ortwine, of Baltimore; has no children.

Fifth.—Julien Clairborne married Bessie Quince, of Wilmington, North Carolina; moved to California, where he died suddenly in 1880, and left no children.

Sixth.—Fanny Page living (1886) unmarried.

Seventh.—Hennie Hunter married Bettie Gouldman, and has two daughters, named Fanny Russell and Mary Page.

OBSERVATIONS.

Mrs. Robinson is living at date (1886) at the family seat, called Mount Pisgah, with her daughter, Miss Fanny Page Robinson.

This property, consisting of mansion and 400 to 500 acres of land, belonged to Captain Thomas Robinson's father, Beverly Robinson. The house is one of the finest in the county, and it is situated near the head of Mattaponi Valley, about a quarter of a mile from the river, which divides King William County from King and Queen County, and is seven miles above King William Court House, and five miles below Aylett's, which before the war was quite a town, but was burned at that time, and has never recovered its prosperity.

All Major Thomas Robinson's sons served during the Civil War, and one of them was in prison on Johnson's Island two years. Benjamin died in 1886, aged forty-seven years.

Major Thomas Robinson died July 20, 1855.

RECORD NO. 17
(Supplied by Mrs. Robinson.)

Benjamin Franklin Dabney, eighth child of George Dabney and Susan L. Quarles, and his wife, Sarah Cary Nelson, daughter of Thomas Cary Nelson, of Bleak Hill.

SIXTH GENERATION.

First.—Benjamin. He was placed in the United States army before the war, and fought on the side of the North during the war, and was probably killed.

Second.—Virginia not married, and living (1886).

Third.—May Dacre married Mr. Turner, a deaf mute. They

are living in Mattaponi, King and Queen County, Virginia, and have children.

Fourth.—Sallie Cary, married, and has children, and lives in Henrico County, Virginia.

Fifth.—Lucy, married, and has children. She also resides in Henrico County, Virginia.

Sixth.—Maria, married, and dead; had no children.

OBSERVATIONS.

Benjamin Franklin Dabney was educated at William and Mary's College, and was a fine lawyer. He was Commonwealth Attorney for many years, and until his death, and he also represented his county in the Virginia Legislature for many years.

RECORD NO. 18

(Given by Mrs. Robinson.)

Agnes Dandridge Dabney, ninth child of George Dabney and Susan L. Quarles, married first her cousin, Dr. George Augustus Spiller. He died in early life, leaving a daughter, who died young.

SIXTH GENERATION.

Mrs. Spiller then married a second husband, Mr. Boughton, and about 1840-1, they moved to Missouri; their children were:

SIXTH GENERATION.

First.—Susan D. married Mr. Ellis, and they are living on a farm (1886), sixty miles from Kansas City, Missouri. They had six children—four girls and two boys.

Second.—Bettie C. married Mr. Grant, and lives in Kansas City, Missouri (1886.) They have three children—two boys and a girl. The latter is married, and has one child.

Third.—Virginia B., born about 1836. Married Mr. Millar, a civil engineer, and lives in Kansas City, Missouri. They have one daughter named Agnes D., born in 1873.

OBSERVATIONS.

Mr. Boughton died in 1866. This record was supplied by Mrs. Virginia B. Millar in a letter to Mrs. Maria Hoomes Turner, dated in Kansas City, Missouri, December 1, 1880.

RECORD NO. 19

(Supplied by Mrs. Robinson.)

Dr. John Taliaferro, M. D., and Frances Anderson Dabney, tenth child of George Dabney and Susan L. Quarles.

SIXTH GENERATION.

First.—Emily married Richard H. Waring; he died and left her with two sons and one daughter, who married Peele Dilland. The oldest son, Lowry, married Lucy Fauntleroy, daughter of Dr. Moore Fauntleroy; she died early, and left him with four children.

Second.—John married Miss White, of Alexandria; she died many years since, leaving a daughter, who is now grown up (1886).

Third.—George married Sarah Claughton (pronounced Claton) of Alexandria; her brother, Hiram, is a lawyer, of high standing.

Mrs. Taliaferro married a second time Custis Carter. They had no children, and both are now dead (1886).

RECORD NO. 20

(Supplied by Mrs. Robinson.)

James Lyons Dabney married Elizabeth Washington Dade. He was the thirteenth child of George Dabney and Susan L. Quarles. He was named for the great Richmond lawyer. His wife was the daughter of Major Dade, of Fauquier County, Virginia, whose wife was a Lewis, and a near relative of George Washington. They moved about 1836-7 to Mississippi, and later to Texas, and they had many children, who are all living in Texas (1886.) Mr. J. L. Dabney is still living at this date.

Children are sixth generation.

RECORD NO. 21

(Given by Mrs. Robinson.)

Thomas Smith Dabney, fourteenth child of George Dabney and Susan L. Quarles, married Rebecca Dylees. They had one son, named George, married and living in Pennsylvania, and two daughters, both married and living in Missouri.

SIXTH GENERATION.

Mr. Dabney was a graduate in medicine at Jefferson Medical College, Philadelphia. He moved to Liberty County, Missouri, about 1838, at the same time as his sisters, Agnes D. Boughton and Elizabeth Camp Dabney, and was still living in Clay County, Missouri, in 1880.

RECORD NO. 22
(Given by Mrs. Robinson.)

William N. Turner and Maria Hoomes Dabney, sixteenth child of George Dabney and Susan L. Quarles.

N. B.—They were cousins.

SIXTH GENERATION.

First.—William James married Miss Hawkins, of Stanton, Virginia; she died, leaving one son and one daughter.

Second.—Logan married Miss Peck, and lives in Stanton; they have no children.

Third.—George Dabney.

Fourth.—Benjamin West, named after the great painter, who was a near relative of his grandmother, Susan L. Quarles.

Fifth.—Thomas Smith, living (1886); unmarried.

Sixth.—Oscar married and lives in New York; no children.

Seventh.—Mary Eleanor married Alexander Haynes; she died, leaving two sons and two daughters.

Eighth.—Alice married Dr. Hill; he died, leaving one son. Mrs. Hill married second time her cousin, Fendal Gregory, a lawyer in King William County, Virginia; they had four daughters; (she is now dead).

Ninth.—Cora.

Tenth.—Maria Blair married Kenny Brown, of Augusta, and has children.

And three others who died in infancy.

After the war Mr. Turner moved to Stanton, Virginia, where he died in 1886. Two of his sons, aged twenty-eight and twenty-four years, were killed on a railroad.

CHART OF THOMAS SMITH GREGORY DABNEY'S
DESCENDANTS.

5th Generation.	6th Generation.
Thomas Smith G. Dabney.	
Mary A. Tyler.	1. Benjamin A. Dabney.
	2. Samuel Tyler Dabney.
	3. Charles Dabney.
	4. Thomas Dabney.
	5. James Dabney.
	6. Charles Dabney 2d.
	7. Virginius Dabney.
	8. Edward Dabney.
	9. Sarah Dabney.
	10. Susan D. Dabney.
	11. Sophia D. Dabney.
	12. Benjamin Dabney.
	13. Emmeline Dabney.
	14. Benj. Dabney 2d.
	15. Ida Dabney.
	16. Thomas S. Dabney.
	17. Lelia Dabney.
	18. Rosalie Dabney.
Sophia Hill.	

No. on Chart.	Index.	No. Gen.	No. Record.
7	Virginius Dabney and Miss Mary Heach, and Miss Anna Noland	6	24
14	Benjamin Dabney and MissVirginia Carra-way	6	25
11	Sophia D. Dabney and William Thurmond.	6	26
13	Emmeline Dabney and Benjamin H. Greene	6	28
16	Thomas Smith Dabney, Jr., and Miss Ida May Ewing	6	27

RECORD NO. 23

(Supplied by the late Thomas S. Dabney and his daughter, Mrs. Smedes.)

Thomas Smith Gregory Dabney, fourth child of Benjamin Dabney, and oldest child of same, and his second wife, Sarah Smith, and his first wife, Miss Mary Adelaide Tyler.

SIXTH GENERATION.

First.—Benjamin A., died at the age of nine years.

Second.—Samuel Tyler, died in infancy.

Mrs. Dabney died three years after marriage, in 1823, and three years later, June 22d, 1826, Mr. Dabney married again Miss Sophia Hill. Their children were sixteen, viz.:

Third.—Charles, born March 27th, 1827. He lived only nine months.

Fourth.—Thomas, born December 25th, 1828; died, aged ten years, July 15, 1838.

Fifth.—James, born; died, aged six years, July 9, 1838.

Sixth.—Charles 2d, born; died of yellow fever, September 28, 1853, aged twenty-two years.

Seventh.—Virginius, born at Elmington, February 15th, 1835; married 1st, Miss Maria Heach; married 2d, Miss Anna Noland, living in New York City in 1887.

Eighth.—Edward, born at Burleigh (1836); living at date in New York (1887); unmarried.

Ninth.—Sarah, born at Burleigh, November 4th, 1838; married John R. Eggleston; living at date (1887); no children.

Tenth.—Susan D., born at Burleigh; married Rev. Lyell Smedes, of Raleigh, North Carolina, at Burleigh. He died eleven weeks after; living at date in Dakota (1887).

Eleventh.—Sophia D., born at Burleigh, 1842; married William Thurmond; living a widow in Washington at date (1887).

Twelfth.—Benjamin, born; lived only eight days.

Thirteenth.—Emmeline, born at Burleigh, 1848; married Benjamin H. Greene, civil engineer; living in Montana at date (1887).

Fourteenth.—Benjamin 2d, born at Burleigh, November 4th, 1846; married Virginia Carraway; living at date (1887), at Bonham, Texas.

Fifteenth.—Ida, born in Burleigh, 1848; living unmarried at date (1887).

Sixteenth.—Thomas S. 2d, born in Burleigh, May, 1850; married Miss Ida May Ewing; living at date in Washington, District of Columbia, 1887.

Seventeenth.—Lelia, born in Burleigh, 1852; living at date in Dakota; unmarried (1887).

Eighteenth.—Rosalie, born in Burleigh, 1854; died, aged two months.

Mrs. Mary A. Tyler Dabney was the daughter of Chancellor Samuel Tyler, of Williamsburg. There was but one Chancellor of Virginia at that time, and the position necessarily implied eminence as a lawyer, and integrity as a man, and both of these he possessed in an eminent degree.

The following sketch of Thomas S. Dabney, is compiled from " Memorials of a Southern Planter," a life of her father, written by Mrs. Susan Dabney Smedes:

" Thomas Smith Gregory Dabney was born at Bellevue, his father's seat on the Pamunky River, in King and Queen County, Virginia, on the 4th of January, 1798. His father died when he was only eight years of age, and when nine years old he was placed under the care of his uncle, Dr. John Augustus Smith, then residing in New York, together with his younger brother, Augustine, and the two boys were placed by their uncle at a boarding school in Elizabeth, New Jersey. Thomas did not remain there long, but was taken into the house of his uncle in New York, and sent to a day school. Being too fond of play, his uncle to punish him, placed him at a printer's to learn that occupation, and he there printed a Bible before he came to the conclusion that studying was pleasanter than printing, and begged to be allowed to return to his studies. While living with his uncle he learned enough of surgery to be of lasting benefit to him afterwards.

"When the war of 1812 commenced, and an attack was threatened by the British at Old Point Comfort, his mother's overseer was drafted, and as his going would have been a very serious loss to her, Thomas, who was then at home, and only fourteen years of age, was allowed to go in his place, at which he was much delighted. His mother gave him a lame horse to ride, saying that a lame horse was good enough to advance on, but would not do for a retreat; but he had no chance to show his prowess, for at the end of three weeks, it being evident that the danger had passed, he returned home. He and his brother, Augustine, were then sent to William and Mary's College, their uncle, Dr. J. A. Smith, being at that time the President, but Thomas remained there but a short time, being called to take charge of " Elmington," the family seat, in consequence of his mother having married Colonel James H. Macon, and moved to his home at Mount Prospect, in Kent County, Virginia.

"On June 6th, 1820, at the age of twenty-two, Thomas was married to Miss Mary Adelaide Tyler, a daughter of Chancellor Samuel Tyler, of Williamsburg, Virginia. She lived only three years, and died, leaving two children, one of which died in infancy, and the other at the age of nine years.

" Three years after the death of his first wife, he married a second time Miss Sophia Hill, a daughter of Charles Hill, of King and Queen County, on the 22d day of June, 1826. Here in his beautiful home of " Elmington," on the banks of the North River, Gloucester County, he passed nine years, keeping open house, and dispensing a broad hospitality to all around. His nearest neighbor and most valued friend was his father's half brother, Dr. James Dabney, the owner of the adjoining estate, called the " Exchange," where an equally liberal hospitality prevailed.

" In 1835 he resolved to remove to Mississippi. He purchased in Hinds County in that State, 4,000 acres of land, to which he removed with his family and all his slaves, his son, Virginius, being then an infant in arms. He was accompanied by his brother Augustine and family, and other relatives and friends, all of whom settled near him in Mississippi. Here he became a successful cotton planter on a large scale, and created a model plantation, and a model house which he named " Burleigh," and here he passed very many years, varying it with a summer every year at Pass Christian, where he bought a house for the purpose. Here in Mississippi most of his remaining children were born.

" In 1853 he had the great misfortune to lose his oldest son, Charles, by yellow fever, contracted at Pass Christian, a highly gifted and promising young man of twenty-two years, who had just graduated at the law school of Harvard University. This was a heavy blow to him, but a still greater one to his beloved wife, who never recovered from it, and in 1861 she died, just as the Civil War commenced, and the State seceded.

" Mr. Dabney was an Old Line Whig, and resisted secession as long as possible, but when it became inevitable, he cast in his lot with his adopted State, and went with it. Three of his sons, the youngest only fourteen years of age, shouldered their muskets, joined the Confederate army, and served throughout the war, and all lived to come back again after it was finished. At the Fall of Vicksburg, the Northern Army over-ran Mr. Dabney's plantation, pillaging and destroying, and the family had to leave it, going first to Mobile, and afterwards to Macon, Georgia, where they remained until the war was over.

"In the autumn of 1864 they moved back to "Burleigh," having been refugees from it for a year and a half. Mr. Dabney set himself to work to repair his shattered fortunes, but reverses again overtook him, and in 1882 he was obliged to leave his beloved "Burleigh" forever, and move to Baltimore, where he spent the remaining days of his life.

"He died very suddenly, and without any warning, on the first day of March, 1885, universally mourned, not only by his children and grandchildren, who idolized him, but by every one who knew him."—(*From Mrs. Smedes' Book*.")

From several obituaries which appeared, I select the following, taken from the *New Orleans Daily City Item*, of March 5th, 1885:

"The death is announced at his residence in Baltimore, of Colonel Thomas Smith Dabney, long one of the most distinguished citizens and cotton planters of Mississippi. Colonel Dabney had reached the venerable age of eighty-seven, and his death was peaceful, as becomes that of a man who leaves behind him only the most honorable memories of a life worthily and usefully spent.

"A Virginian by birth—he was born in Gloucester County in that State—he was the descendant, both through his paternal and maternal line from ancestry who were prominent figures in the ranks of the cultured, and the affluent society of Colonial Virginia. From them he inherited those virtues, some of them Spartan in their simplicity, which emphasized his character; for inflexible as he was in will and purpose, all who knew him—and his circle of acquaintances was wide indeed—recognized in him a touching faith in his fellow man, which beautified, and gilded as it were, those virile traits which marked him as a man in ten thousand. It is rare indeed that there are united in one man those delicately blended characteristics of gentleness, and an iron will, which were so specially the features of Colonel Dabney's nature;

and if he was at times deceived in his trust, it did not lessen his faith in the honesty and goodness of man.

"Colonel Dabney removed many years ago from Virginia to Mississippi, and settled in Hinds County, where, having purchased land, he commenced the cultivation of cotton on an extensive scale. He formed one of a small colony of Virginia settlers, who about the same time also removed to that County, and established themselves there as cotton planters. This colony brought with them, to the then comparatively new country of that part of Mississippi, the elegance and hospitality of the Old Dominion, in whose highest schools of dignity and social worth they had been reared.

"At "Burleigh," as Colonel Dabney named his plantation, about nine miles from Raymond, after Queen Elizabeth's astute minister, the old time courtesy of Virginia, the unaffected ease and liberal spirit of welcome reigned supreme. Its hospitable doors were always open to the friends of its large hearted owner, and in the society of those friends, and of his neighbors, of a devoted and amiable wife, and of a large family of children—most of whom survive to revere their father's memory--this exemplary Virginian of the old school—a school which now, alas! numbers but few surviving adepts—passed his days for nearly two generations, in the lap of prosperity.

Colonel Dabney possessed many friends and acquaintances in this city, especially before the war. During the summer season it was his wont to seek the shores of Mississippi Sound with his family, and to Pass Christian, where he owned a handsome residence, he transferred for a time, annually, that genial hospitality which he had brought to "Burleigh" from the home of his fathers in Virginia.

"A man of culture and liberal education, of generous impulses and warm heartedness, which grew cold only at any suggestion that might have affected his innate pride and his dignity; he was one whom men at once loved and respected, whose word was his bond, and who, dying without reproach in the face of the world, has left behind him a name to which his children and his descendants may look back with pride, and upon which all good men may pattern."

The late Thomas S. Dabney, writing of his son-in-law, Mr. J. H. Eggleston, who was in the Confederate navy during the Civil War, and a lieutenant on board the "Merrimac" when she destroyed the "Congress" frigate, after Admiral Buchanan had been wounded, and the Merrimac was in command of Lieutenant Catesby Ap Jones, says:

"My son-in-law was in command of the red hot battery, and when Commodore Jones ran under the stern of the "Congress," then aground, he ordered Lieutenant Eggleston to do his duty; this meant but one thing, and made his blood run cold. He looked in and saw his old messmates, with whom he had had many a frolic, and whom he was now called upon inexorably to slay. He gave the word and they were in fragments; the ship was set on fire and burned to the water's edge with her dead and wounded. What a war!"

RECORD NO. 24

(Given by Mrs. Smedes.)

Virginius Dabney, fifth son of Thomas Smith Gregory Dabney, and his wife, Sophia Hill, and his first wife, Miss Maria Heach.

SEVENTH GENERATION.

First.—Richard Heach.

Mrs. Dabney died soon after, and he married again Miss Anna Noland. Their children were :

Second.—Thomas Lloyd.

Third.—Noland.

Fourth.—Virginius.

Fifth.—Joseph Drexel.

Sixth.—Susan.

F

OBSERVATIONS.

Virginius Dabney was born in Virginia, and was an infant in arms when his father moved to Mississippi. When the Civil War commenced he joined the Confederate army, and served throughout the war, in which he was wounded. He was on General Lee's staff, and with him at the surrender at Appomattox, and on the morning of that day, shared with his General, by his command, his very frugal breakfast. After the war he opened a classic school in New York, which he still continues, assisted by his brother Edward. He is an author, and wrote a novel called "Don Miff," which is well known and very popular in the South.

RECORD NO. 25

(Supplied by Mrs. Smedes.)

Benjamin, eighth son of Thomas Smith Gregory Dabney, and Sophia Hill, and his wife, Miss Virginia Carraway.

SEVENTH GENERATION.

First.—Benjamin.
Second.—Charles.
Third.—Ward.
Fourth.—Edward.
Fifth.—Virginia.
Mr. Dabney is a physician, and resides in Bonham, Texas.

RECORD NO. 26

(Supplied by Mrs. Smedes.)

William Thurmond and Sophia Dabney, third daughter of Thomas Smith Gregory Dabney, and Sophia Hill.

SEVENTH GENERATION.

First.—Sophia Dabney.
Mrs. Thurmond is living at date (1887), in Washington, District of Columbia.

(Supplied by Mrs. Smedes.)

Thomas Smith Dabney, Jr., M. D., youngest son of Thomas Smith Gregory Dabney, and Sophia Hill, and his wife, Miss Ida May Ewing.

SEVENTH GENERATION.

Thomas Burleigh.

Dr. Thomas S. Dabney is a physician, and resides in Kansas City, Missouri.

RECORD NO. 28

(Supplied by Mrs. Smedes.)

Benjamin H. Greene and Emmeline Dabney, fourth daughter of Thomas S. Dabney, and Sophia Hill.

SEVENTH GENERATION.

First.—Thomas.

Second.—Emmeline.

Third.—Sophia.

Mr. Greene is a civil engineer, and is residing (1887) in Montana.

RECORD NO. 29

(Given by Mrs. Smedes.)

Augustine Lee Dabney, second son of Benjamin Dabney and Sarah Smith.

Mr. Augustine Lee Dabney married first Ann Robinson. She died, leaving no children. He married a second time, Elizabeth Smith, and they had four sons and five daughters, viz.:

SIXTH GENERATION.

First.—Frederick Yeamans, who married Agatha Moncure.

Second.—Thomas Gregory married Fanny Bowmar.

Third.—Marye married Elizabeth Marshall. Is a lawyer living in Mississippi; has one daughter (Susan).

Fourth.—John Davis married first Virginia Meade. She died, leaving no children. He then married Virginia Grant.

Fifth.—Ann Robinson, living at date (1887), unmarried.

Sixth.—Elizabeth, married Judge W. W. Porter, and is living in Santa Rosa, California.

Seventh.—Martha Chamberlayne, living at date, unmarried.

Eighth.—Mary Smith married William Ware; had one son, Sedley. He is dead, and she resides in Mississippi.

Ninth.—Letitia married T. Marshall Miller, a lawyer, and lives in Vicksburg, Mississippi, and has one son named Raymond.

OBSERVATIONS.

Judge Augustine Lee Dabney moved from Virginia to Mississippi with his brother Thomas, in 1835. In 1877, he again moved from Mississippi to California with his wife and two daughters, and there died in 1879, at the age of seventy-nine years, of appoplexy.

Mr. Augustine Lee Dabney was a boy at school in Elizabeth, New Jersey, and afterwards was educated at William and Mary's College. He married Miss Elizabeth Smith, and established himself in Gloucester County, Virginia, some miles back from his brother Thomas, where he remained until he removed to Mississippi. He established himself at Raymond, Mississippi, nine miles from his brother Thomas, at "Burleigh," and soon obtained a great reputation as a lawyer, and was for eight years Judge of the Probate Court of Hinds County. He was distinguished for the same hospitality and lavish generosity as his brother Thomas.

CHART OF AUGUSTINE LEE DABNEY'S DESCENDANTS.

5th Generation.	6th Generation.
Augustine Lee Dabney.	1. Frederick Yeamans Dabney.
	2. Thomas Gregory Dabney.
	3. Marye Dabney.
	4. John Davis Dabney.
	5. Ann Robinson Dabney.
	6. Elizabeth Dabney.
	7. Martha Chamberlayne Dabney.
	8. Mary Smith Dabney.
	9. Letitia Dabney.
Elizabeth Smith.	

RECORD NO. 30.

(Given by Mrs. Smedes.)

Frederick Yeamans Dabney, oldest son of Augustine Lee Dabney and Elizabeth Smith, and his wife, Agatha Moncure.

SEVENTH GENERATION.

First.—Moncure.

Second.—Augustine Lee.

Third.—Frederick Conway.

Fourth.—Evelyn.

Fifth.—Susan.

Sixth.—Agatha.

Mr. Frederick Y. Dabney was Colonel of Engineers in the Confederate army.

OBSERVATIONS.

Mr. Frederick Y. Dabney is a civil engineer, and resides in Mississippi (1887).

RECORD NO. 31

(Given by Mrs. Smedes.)

Thomas Gregory Dabney, second son of Augustine Dabney and Elizabeth Smith, and his wife, Fanny Bowmar.

SEVENTH GENERATION.

First.—Augustine.

Second.—Bowmar.

Third.—Thomas.

Fourth.—James.

Fifth.—Elizabeth.

Sixth.—Fanny.

Seventh.—Frederick Marye.

OBSERVATIONS.

Mr. Thomas G. Dabney is a civil engineer, and is residing at present time (1886), in Memphis, Tennessee.

RECORD NO. 32

(Given by Mrs. Smedes.)

John Davis Dabney, fourth son of Judge Augustine Dabney and Elizabeth Smith, and his wife (his second wife) Virginia Grant.

N. B.—There were no children by his first wife, Virginia Meade.

SEVENTH GENERATION.

First.—John.

Second.—John.

Third.—Marye.

Fourth.—Malcolm.

OBSERVATIONS.

Dr. John Davis Dabney is a physician, and resides in Mississippi.

RECORD NO. 33

(Given by Mrs. Smedes.)

Judge W. W. Porter and Elizabeth Dabney, second daughter of Augustine Lee Dabney, and Elizabeth Smith.

SEVENTH GENERATION.

First.—Ellen.

Second.—Harriet.

Third.—Elizabeth.

Fourth.—Alice.

Fifth.—Ann Marye.

OBSERVATIONS.

Mr. Porter is a lawyer, and resides in Santa Rosa, California.

RECORD NO. 34

(Given by Mrs. Smedes.)

T. Marshall Millar and Letitia Dabney, fifth daughter of Augustine Lee Dabney, and Elizabeth Smith.

SEVENTH GENERATION.

First.—Frederick Dabney.

Second.—Marshall.

Third.—John.

Fourth.—Van Dorn.

Fifth.—Raymond.

OBSERVATIONS.

Mr. Millar is a leading lawyer in Vicksburg, Mississippi.

RECORD NO. 35
(Given by Mrs. Smedes.)

Dr. Lewis Chamberlayne and Martha Dabney, daughter of Benjamin Dabney and Sarah Smith.

SIXTH GENERATION.

First.—John Hampden married Mary Gibson; died in Richmond in 1882.

Second.—Parke, C. married George Bagby, the humorist, and is living in Richmond, a widow.

OBSERVATIONS.

Dr. Chamberlayne was a lineal descendant of John Hampden. Both he and Mrs. Chamberlayne are dead.

John Hampden Chamberlayne, their son, was a talented young journalist, of Richmond, Virginia, who died quite young, universally lamented.

RECORD NO. 36
(Given by Mrs. Robinson.)

Dr. James Dabney, son of George Dabney, of Dabney's Ferry, and his first wife. They had only one child, a son, named Benjamin Franklin Dabney, who went to live in Mississippi. Dr. James Dabney married a second wife, Miss Perrin. Their children were:

FIFTH GENERATION.

First.—James, who married Miss Emory Tabb.

Second.—Thomas.

Dr. James Dabney lived near his brother, Major Thomas Dabney, from ten to fifteen miles distant. Major Thomas Dabney's place was called the "Donnell," Dr. James Dabney's place was called the "Greenville." Mrs. Robinson, who gives this record, says that she remembers seeing her grand-uncle James, at the "Donnell," (where she often visited when a child) coming in his sulky, the only way in which old gentlemen traveled in those days, and that she remembers seeing him again, when she was about fourteen or fifteen years of age, at the house of a cousin in Gloucester, whom she was visiting. Mr. James Dabney, his son, lived in Gloucester, at his seat called the "Exchange."

RECORD NO. 37

(Given by Mrs. Robinson.)

James Dabney, son of Dr. James Dabney, and his second wife, Miss Perrin, and his wife, Miss Emory Tabb.

SIXTH GENERATION.

First.—James.

Second.—Thomas Todd.

Third.—Franklin.

Fourth.—William.

Fifth.—Lucy, who married James Duncan, and has two daughters, named Emory and Mary.

Sixth.—James Lee.

Seventh.—Evelyn.

OBSERVATIONS.

Mr. James Dabney is living at this date (1886) on the family estate in Gloucester, called the "Exchange."

RECORD NO. 38

(Given by Mrs. Robinson.)

Major Thomas Dabney, son of George Dabney, of Dabney's Ferry, and his second wife, and Miss Lucy Walker, his first wife. They had four sons and three daughters, five of them married.

FIFTH GENERATION.

First.—John Milton, who married Elizabeth Taylor Moore, and went South.

Second.—Thomas Overton, who was Commonwealth Attorney

of King William County, Virginia, after Benjamin Franklin Dabney's death, and until his own death.

Of the third and fourth we have no records.

Fifth.—Frances Ellen married Mr. Greene, and left no children.

Sixth.—Mary Susan married Samuel Robinson. She died, and left four sons and three daughters. Major Thomas Robinson married her cousin, Mary Eleanor Dabney's oldest daughter.

Seventh.—Ann Eliza, who married Mr. Sizer. She died young, leaving one son, who is now living (1886).

Major Thomas Dabney married a second time Mary Eleanor Tompkins. They had two sons—James, who killed himself accidentally while hunting, at fifteen years of age, and Alexander, who was killed in the Civil war. Major Thomas Dabney lived in King William County, Virginia, at his place called the "Donnell." He died over thirty years since, aged over seventy years. He was an able and hardworking lawyer.

RECORD NO. 39

(Given by Mrs. Dabney in letter to Mrs. Smedes, and sent by her to me.)

John Milton Dabney, son of Major Thomas Dabney and Lucy Walker, and his wife, Elizabeth Taylor Moore.

SIXTH GENERATION.

First.—Helen Moore married Dr. Bat Smith, and had three sons, James B. Milton Dabney, and Garland G. (still living in 1886).

Second.—Lucy Walker married Captain James Walker Powell, of the United States army. Living at date (1886).

Third.—William Penn Taylor married Carrie Goodman.

Fourth.—John Scott. Living at date (1886), unmarried.

Fifth.—John Milton, Jr. Living at date (1886).

OBSERVATIONS.

J. Milton Dabney was murdered on his estate, in Mississippi, about the year 1883-4, as per letter of his widow to Mrs. Smedes, dated in Meridian, July 28th, 1884.

Second Branch

OF THE

Virginia Dabneys.

THEY BEING THE DESCENDANTS OF GEORGE DABNEY, THE SON OF
CORNELIUS D'AUBIGNÉ, THE ORIGINAL SETTLER AND HIS
FIRST WIFE BORN IN ENGLAND OR WALES, PRE-
VIOUS TO HIS PARENTS COMING
TO VIRGINIA.

CHART OF GEORGE DABNEY'S DESCENDANTS.

1st Generat'n.	2d Generat'n.	3d Generat'n.	4th Generat'n.	5th Generation.

Cornelius d'Aubigné, Original Emigrant.

First Wife.

Name Unknown.

1. George Dabney, only son.

2. George Dabney 2d.

Wife Unkno'n Wm. Dabney.

Miss Barrett. Sarah Dabney

3. James Dabney.

4. Ann Dabney.

5. George Dabney.

6. Elizabeth Dabney.

7. Cicely Dabney.

8. William Dabney.

9. Pouncey Dabney.

10. Mary Dabney.

11. Charity Dabney.

12. Ann Anderson Dabney.

Judith Anderson.

No. on Chart.	Index.	No. Gen.	No. Record.
1	George Dabney, son of Cornelius d'Aubigné	2	40
2	George Dabney 2nd, son of George Dabney 1st.........................	3	41
3	James Dabney and Judith Anderson.......	4	42
8	William Dabney and Sarah Watson.......	5	43

RECORD NO. 40

(Given by late Rev. Edward Fontaine.)

George Dabney, son of Cornelius d'Aubigné by his first wife, name unknown, and his wife, name also unknown.

THIRD GENERATION.

First.—George.

Second.—Sarah married William Winston, and was the mother of Judge Edmund Winston.

Third.—William married Miss Barrett.

And several daughters.

George Dabney was born in England or Wales previous to the emigration of his parents to this country, and must have been grown to man's estate when he came. He married in Virginia soon after coming over, and was already married when his father, Cornelius d'Aubigné or Dabney married Sarah Jennings or Jennens in 1721.

Charles William Dabney, of Dalton Junction, Hanover County, Virginia, says: "I remember seeing a copy of George Dabney's will, dated in 1744, which I think may be found in the Records of King William County, in which he provides for his sons, George and William, and several daughters," whose names he cannot now recollect.

He also says that "George Dabney was still living when the Revolutionary War began, an old man, and therefore he must have been born about the beginning of the eighteenth century. He was the head of a family about 1740, as he (Charles William Dabney) has a patent of lands, some of which he himself owns now, which was granted to George Dabney at that time by King George II., of England."

RECORD NO. 41

(Supplied by James Watson Dabney, and Dr. William Cecil Dabney,
of Charlottesville, Virginia.)

George Dabney 2nd, son of George Dabney, and grandson of Cornelius d'Aubigné, and his wife, whose name is unknown to me. I only know of one son, viz:

FOURTH GENERATION.

James (Colonel) born January 6th, 1735; married Judith Anderson, February 26th, 1756; died November 13th, 1803.

OBSERVATIONS.

Charles William Dabney, of Dalton Junction, states that he knows James Dabney to be the son of George Dabney 2d, from the will of George Dabney 1st, which he remembers to have seen.

RECORD NO. 42

(Furnished by James Watson Dabney, of Bonham, Texas; corrected by his cousin, Dr. William Cecil Dabney.)

Colonel James Dabney, son of George Dabney 2d, and his wife, Judith Anderson.

FIFTH GENERATION.

First.—Ann, born November, 1757; died in 1758.

Second.—George, born November, 1759; died in same year.

Third.—Elizabeth, born October, 1760; married David Johnson in 1794. Died.

Fourth.—Cicely, born November, 1768.

Fifth.—William, born September, 1771; married Sarah Watson, daughter of James Watson, and Betsey Shelton, April 26, 1792; died October, 1813, and she died same year.

Sixth.—Pouncey, born June, 1774; died November, 1780.

Seventh.—Mary, born January 31, 1777; married Edward Hallam, of Stonington, Connecticut, December 6th, 1794. Died.

Eighth.—Charity, born March, 1779; married Judge Todd, of Virginia, and afterwards of Frankfort, Kentucky. Died.

Ninth.—Ann Anderson, born 1781. Either Ann Anderson, or Cicely, which I don't know, married Major Thomas Shelton.

Colonel James Dabney commanded a company of riflemen in the war of the Revolution. His daughter, Elizabeth, married David Johnson when only fourteen years of age, and went with him to live in South Carolina, and there are grandchildren of hers living in Union, South Carolina. He was judge in South Carolina.

His daughter, Mary, who married Mr. Edward Hallam, of Stonington, Connecticut, had two daughters; one married Mr. William King, of New York, and the other, Harriet, married Mr. William Richardson, of Virginia. They afterwards, in 1854, moved North. Mrs. Richardson is dead, but has a daughter living, Susan Boylston, who married Dr. William R. Donaghe, and lives in Morristown, New Jersey, at the present time (1887.) Mr. King is living at the same place, aged over eighty years.

Mr. Hallam moved from Connecticut to Richmond, Virginia, previous to 1794. He kept the Eagle Hotel in that city, and entertained there General La Fayette, at the time of his visit to Virginia, in 1825.

Dr. William Cecil Dabney states that Charity Dabney married lawyer Todd, of Virginia, and afterwards of Frankfort, Kentucky, and he thinks that she was the mother of Mrs. Abraham Lincoln. But this must be an error, as the following extract of a letter from the Rev. Robert L. Dabney, of the Texas University, Austin, Texas, dated November 30th, 1887, will show. He says:

"Charity Dabney was the youngest child of old Captain James Dabney, and inherited his homestead on Cub Creek, Louisa County, Virginia. She married lawyer Samuel Todd, of Rockbridge County, Virginia. Rev. John Todd, Sr., had come to Louisa County, at the instance of Samuel Davies (the great apostle of Virginia), and was pastor of Captain James Dabney and Mrs. Samuel Dabney and family. His son, Rev. John Todd, Jr., succeeded to his lands, his school, and his pastoral work. An uncle of his, a layman, had settled in Rockbridge County, and lawyer Samuel Todd, was the son of that uncle. He, while at the Todd school in Louisa County pursuing his classical studies, formed an attachment for Charity Dabney, and ultimately married her. Not long after, the Rev. John Todd, Jr., was taken with the Kentucky fever of emigration, and persuaded his cousin Samuel and bride to emigrate with him to that State. My father, Charles Dabney, bought Charity Dabney's homestead in

1811. Samuel Todd and Charity Dabney, his wife, settled near Frankfort, Kentucky. They were *not* the progenitors of Mrs. Abraham Lincoln. Charity Dabney Todd left a son, which son was afterwards Judge Todd, a distinguished lawyer and Circuit Judge, near Frankfort. He left posterity, and his widow was living recently, a superior old lady, with whom I corresponded, and she assured me that Mrs. Lincoln was not a descendant of her husband's mother, but of a distant branch of the family."

Charles W. Dabney states that during the war he was in service with a Dr. Todd, who was a brother of Mrs. Abraham Lincoln.

RECORD NO. 43

(Given by James Watson Dabney and Dr. William Cecil Dabney.)

William Dabney, son of Colonel James Dabney, of Albemarle, and Judith Anderson, and his wife, Sarah Watson.

SIXTH GENERATION.

First—James Watson, born in 1793; died in Florida 1860, unmarried.

Second.—Maria, born in 1794. Married Colonel Samuel Carr, nephew of Thomas Jefferson; died in 1843.

Third.—Mary Senora, born in 1801. Married William B. M. Perkins; died about 1840.

Fourth.—Walter Davis, born in 1803. Married Miss Sappington, of Louisiana. Died in 1850.

Fifth.—William S., born in Dunlora in 1805. Married Mrs. Susan Fitzhugh Greene, *nee* Gordon, of Galloway, Scotland; died in 1865.

Sixth.—Louisa Elizabeth, born in 1807. Married William M. Woods, of Nelson County, Virginia; died in 1843.

OBSERVATIONS.

Mrs. Sarah Watson Dabney was a sister of Dr. George Watson, a leading physician of Richmond, Virginia, and a daughter of James Watson and Betsey Shelton, of Louisa County, Virginia. Colonel Samuel Carr, who married Maria Dabney, was a nephew

G

of President Jefferson. Louisa E. Woods had two children. Sonora (dead), and J. Watson, living (1887), in Memphis, Tennessee. He served in the Fourth Virginia Infantry during the war.

CHART OF WILLIAM DABNEY, OF KING WILLIAM COUNTY, VA.
(SON OF COLONEL JAMES DABNEY, OF ALBEMARLE
COUNTY, VA., AND JUDITH ANDERSON),
AND HIS DESCENDANTS.

5th Generation.	6th Generation..
1. William Dabney.	
	2. James Watson Dabney.
	3. Maria Dabney.
	4. Mary Senora Dabney.
	5. Walter Davies Dabney.
	6. William S. Dabney.
	7. Louise Elizabeth Dabney.
Sarah Watson.	

No. on Chart.	Index.	No. Gen.	No. Record.
1	William Dabney and Sarah Watson........	5	43
3	Maria Dabney and Col. Samuel Carr.......	6	44
4	Mary Senora Dabney and Wm. B. M. Perkins	6	45
5	Walter Davies Dabney and Miss Sappington.................................	6	46
6	William S. Dabney and Mrs. Susan Fitzhugh Green.............	6	47

RECORD NO. 44

(Supplied by James Watson Dabney and Dr. William Cecil Dabney.)

Maria Dabney, daughter of William Dabney and Sarah Watson, and Colonel Samuel Carr.

SIXTH GENERATION,

First.—George Watson. Living (1886).

Second.—Maria Jefferson married Mr. Swayze, and is the mother of M. J. C. Swayze. Living at date (1886), in New Orleans.

Third.—Sarah Dabney married her cousin, Frank E. G. Carr. Is dead, and left one son, George Watson Carr, Jr., who resides in Roanoke County, Virginia.

Colonel Samuel Carr was a nephew of President Thomas Jefferson. Maria Jefferson married first, Mr. Miller, and second, Mr. Swayze, and is living (1887), in New Orleans.

RECORD NO. 45

(Given by James Watson Dabney and Dr. Cecil William Dabney).

Mary Senora Dabney, daughter of William and Sarah Watson Dabney, and William B. M. Perkins.

SIXTH GENERATION.

First.—James, killed in the Union army in the Civil War.

Second.—Sarah married Mr. Bookers. Died in 1884, and left two children.

Third.—Mildred, living; unmarried in 1886.

RECORD NO. 46

(Supplied by J. W. Dabney, Dr. Wm. Cecil Dabney, and James Watson Woods, of Memphis.)

Walter Davis Dabney, son of William and Sarah Watson Dabney, and Miss Sappington, of New Orleans.

SIXTH GENERATION.

First.—James Watson, born 1840, living in Bonham, Texas, in 1886.

Second.—John H. died in the Southern army, in the Civil War

Third.—Louisianna Sappington still living (1886.) Married Mr. Lewis, of Virginia, and has a large family.

Fourth.—Edward Moon, killed in Confederate army, in 1863, at Fredericksburg.

Mr. Walter Davis Dabney settled in or near Memphis, Tennessee, where he lived in luxury before the Civil War. His son, James Watson Dabney, served four years in the Confederate army, and now is in business in Bonham, Texas. John H. Dabney died in a Federal prison in Chicago, having been taken prisoner. Captain Edward Moon Dabney commanded the Thirty-first Regiment of Infantry when he was killed at Fredericksburg in 1863.

RECORD NO. 47

(Given by Dr. William Cecil Dabney.)

William Dabney, son of William and Sarah Watson Dabney, and his wife, Susan Fitzhugh Greene, *nee* Gordon.

SIXTH GENERATION.

First.—Bazil Gordon, born about 1847-8; killed in battle in 1865, at the age of seventeen years.

Second.—Dr. William Cecil, living in Charlottesville, Virginia, in 1886.

Third.—Walter Davis died in infancy.

Fourth.—Walter 2d, a lawyer, and in the Virginia Legislature in 1886.

Fifth.—Sarah Watson died in infancy.

Sixth.—Maria Gordon married Mr. Moon, and is living at date near Charlottesville, 1887.

Seventh.—Samuel Gordon was educated in Europe. He is at present (1886) Professor of Physiology in Louisville, Kentucky, and was married December 21, 1887, to Miss Louisa K. Allen, daughter of Buckner Allen, Louisville.

OBSERVATIONS.

Mrs. Susan F. G. Dabney is living at date in Charlottesville, Virginia; she was born in Galloway, Scotland.

Dr. William Cecil Dabney is married, and has four daughters.

Walter Dabney has one daughter; he is a Professor in the University of Virginia.

Mrs. Maria Gordon (Dabney) Moon has three daughters and one son.

RECORD NO. 48
(Given by Rev. Edward Fontaine.)

William Winston and Sarah Dabney, a daughter of George Dabney 1st, son of Cornelius d'Aubigné by his first wife.

FOURTH GENERATION.

First.—Judge Edmund.

Second.—Daughter married Colonel Peter Fontaine.

Third.—Daughter married Dr. Walker.

OBSERVATIONS.

Rev. J. Blair Dabney, in his record, says: "I know that Colonel William Dabney had a sister who intermarried with Mr. Wiliam Winston; she was the mother of Judge Edmund Winston, who was a Judge of the General Court."

This William Winston may have been a son of the Colonel William Winston, of Langaloo and Rockcastle, who married Elizabeth Dabney, daughter of John d'Aubigné, the original settler, brother to Cornelius d'Aubigné, as stated by Rev. Edward Fontaine. Mr. John Dabney, of Salem, Virginia, concurs with me in this surmise.

RECORD NO. 49
(Taken from J. Blair Dabney Records.)

William Dabney, son of George Dabney 1st, known as William Dabney, of Aldringham, and his wife, Miss Barrett.

FOURTH GENERATION.

First.—George married Elizabeth Price; died in 1824, aged eighty years.

Second.—Charles, Colonel of Dabney's Legion in the war of the Revolution, died unmarried 1830, aged eighty-five years.

Third.—Samuel married Miss Merriwether, of Albemarle. Died.

Fourth.—Robert or Robin-married Miss Barbara Winston. Died.

Fifth.—Elizabeth married William Morris, of Hanover County, Virginia.

Sixth.—Susanna died, unmarried.

OBSERVATIONS.

William Dabney had his property in the upper part of Hanover and the lower part of Louisa Counties, Virginia, on the South Anna River. He must have been born somewhere between 1725-30, not after. He married Miss Barrett, a daughter of the Rev. —— Barrett, one of the Faculty of William and Mary's College.

William Dabney and his wife were both dead when the Revolutionary War commenced, although William Dabney's father was still living then, a very old man.

CHART OF WILLIAM DABNEY, OF ALDRINGHAM (SON OF GEORGE DABNEY 1ST,) AND HIS DESCENDANTS.

3d Generation.	4th Generation.
1. William Dabney.	
	2. George Dabney.
	3. Charles Dabney.
	4. Samuel Dabney.
	5. Robert Dabney.
	6. Elizabeth Dabney.
	7. Susanna Dabney.
Miss Barrett.	

No. on Chart.	Index.	No. Gen.	No. Record.
1	William Dabney and Miss Barrett.........	3	49
2	George Dabney and Elizabeth Price.......	4	50
3	Charles Dabney's Memoir.................	4	65
4	Samuel Dabney and Miss Merriwether....	4	66
5	Robert or Robin Dabney and Miss Winston	4	73
6	Elizabeth Dabney and Wm. Morris........	4	80

RECORD NO. 50

(Taken from J. Blair Dabney Records.)

Captain George Dabney, son of William Dabney and Miss Barrett, and his wife, Elizabeth Price.

FIFTH GENERATION.

First.—William married Miss Hylton, of Richmond.

Second.—George died, unmarried.

Third.—Mary died, unmarried.

Fourth.—Nancy married Judge Alexander Stuart.

Fifth.—Maria died, unmarried.

Sixth.—John married Susanna D. Morris.

Seventh.—Lucy B. died unmarried in 1810; she was very lovely and fascinating.

Eighth.—Elizabeth married first, Lynn Shackleford; married second, William Pollard. She was also very beautiful.

Ninth.—Jane died unmarried about 1835.

Tenth.—Catherine married Seaton Grantland, Member of Congress from Georgia, late in life, and had no children; she died about 1845; she was a great beauty, and highly gifted and educated.

Eleventh.—Chiswell married first, Miss Norvell; married second, Mrs. Nancy Wyatt; married third, Mrs. Elizabeth Lee, *nee* Tabb.

OBSERVATIONS.

Mr. George Dabney died in 1824. Mrs. Dabney's mother was a Randolph.

Mr. John Blair Dabney in his book of Records and Memoirs of his branch of the Dabney family, says: "I give Captain

George Dabney the title of " Captain," although it was only in the Militia, because in Revolutionary times these military designations signified something more than mere appellations of honor and distinction. They were often badges of real service, and when the whole power of the country was constantly required for its defence, were generally assumed from motives of patriotism."

Captain George Dabney was Captain of Dabney's Legion, which was commanded by his young brother, Charles. Their services ended at the surrender of Cornwallis at Yorktown. They afterwards received the thanks of Congress for their distinguished services, as may be seen in the Preface of Wirt's Life of Patrick Henry.

The following is cut from an old newspaper, respecting the powder gourd used by Captain George Dabney in the war: "Andrew Russell, of Clinton County, Kentucky, has the old powder gourd of Captain George Dabney, an old soldier of the Revolution. This little gourd is dyed red, and has a crooked handle, with small wooden pegs, to which was tied the flax string that supported some of the powder that dealt destruction to the foes of American freedom, and helped establish our country.

" Captain Dabney some time before the war had undertaken the superintendence of the numerous and extensive estates of General Thomas Nelson, one of the signers of the Declaration of Independence, and afterwards Governor of Virginia.

" He was a staunch and uncompromising supporter of the Republican party, but never manifested any disposition to engage in public life. His tastes were essentially domestic, and it was in the shades of private life that his finer qualities took root, flourished and expanded.

" Patrick Henry was his intimate friend and neighbor, and from him Mr. Wirt obtained much of the information which he has embodied in his life of Patrick Henry.

"Captain Dabney died on his farm in Hanover County, called the " Grove," in the summer of 1824, at the extreme old age of

eighty years. On this farm he had been born, bred, and resided all
his long life. His house had passed into the hands of strangers
before 1850. The Rev. John Blair was his intimate friend."

CHART OF CAPTAIN GEORGE DABNEY, OF REVOLUTIONARY MEM-
ORY, (OLDEST SON OF WILLIAM DABNEY AND MISS
BARRETT,) AND HIS WIFE ELIZABETH
PRICE'S DESCENDANTS.

4th Generation.	5th Generation.
1. Captain George Dabney.	
	2. William Dabney.
	3. George Dabney,
	4. Mary Dabney.
	5. Nancy Dabney.
	6. Maria Dabney.
	7. John Dabney.
	8. Lucy B. Dabney.
	9. Elizabeth Dabney.
	10. Jane Dabney.
	11. Catherine Dabney.
	12. Chiswell Dabney.

Elizabeth Price.

No. on Chart.	Index.	No. Gen.	No. Record.
1	Captain George Dabney and Elizabeth Price	4	50
2	William Dabney and Mehetable Hylton....	6	51
	Martha Dabney and Jefferson Stuart.......	7	52
5	Nancy Dabney and Judge Alexander Stuart	6	53
	Archibald Stuart and Elizabeth Pannell...	7	54
7	John Dabney and Susanna Morris.........	6	55
	John Blair Dabney and Elizabeth Lewis Towles..............................	7	56
9	Elizabeth Dabney and Lynn Shackelford..	6	62
12	Chiswell Dabney and Miss Norvell........	6	63
	Elizabeth Dabney and John S. Langhorne..	7	64

RECORD NO. 51

(Taken from the J. Blair Dabney Records.)

William Dabney, oldest son of Captain George Dabney and Elizabeth Price, and his wife, Mehetable Hylton.

SIXTH GENERATION.

First.—Martha married Jefferson Stuart, son of Judge Archibald Stuart.

Second.—Sarah died, unmarried.

Third.—Lucy married Dr. Whorton, and had several children.

Fourth.—William Beverly married Miss Norvell, and had two sons, William A., who married Miss Emily Nelson, and Charles, who married her sister, Miss Page Nelson.

Fifth.—Nancy married Judge Alexander Stuart, and was the mother of Archibald Stuart and Nancy Stuart.

OBSERVATIONS.

William Dabney was a merchant in Richmond, Virginia.

RECORD NO. 52

(J. Blair Dabney Records.)

Jefferson Stuart and Martha Dabney, a daughter of William Dabney and Mehetable Hylton.

SIXTH GENERATION.

First.—William, a Colonel in the Civil War, and was killed.

Second.—Briscoe, who committed suicide.

Mrs. Stuart was one of the excellent of the earth, and died about 1850. He was from Augusta, Virginia.

Lucy Dabney, another daughter of William and Mehetable Dabney, married Dr. Whorton, of Richmond, Virginia, and was living a widow in Danville at the time J. Blair Dabney wrote his manuscript.

RECORD NO. 53
(J. Blair Dabney Records.)

Judge Alexander Stuart and Nancy Dabney, daughter of Captain George Dabney, and Miss Barrett.

FIFTH GENERATION.

First.—Archibald married Miss Elizabeth Pannell.

Second.—Nancy married Judge J. E. Brown, of Wythe County, and left one son, who died early, and one daughter, who died unmarried.

RECORD NO. 54
(J. Blair Dabney Records.)

Archibald Stuart, son of Nancy Stuart, *nee* Dabney, and his wife, Elizabeth Pannell.

SIXTH GENERATION.

First.—William A. married first, Miss Carter, and second, a widow, whose maiden name was Spiller, and has a numerous family.

Second.—John Dabney, who died, leaving a large family.

Third.—General J. E. B., General in the Confederate army, well known for his fine qualities and bravery, and who was killed in the Civil War, leaving several daughters.

OBSERVATIONS.

Mr. J. Blair Dabney says: " Mr. Archibald Stuart possessed a fine natural capacity, and was a member of two successive conventions in Virginia, and was for many years in the State Senate. He left a large family, of which William A. Stuart has been the most successful."

(Taken from J. Blair Dabney Records.)

John Dabney, sixth child and third son of Captain **George
Dabney** and Miss **Barrett**, and his wife, **Susanna D. Morris.**

FIFTH GENERATION.

First.—John Blair married Elizabeth Lewis Towles; born
about 1793; died April, 1868.

Second.—George Edward married Miss **Cornelia Price, and**
died in 1868, without issue.

Third.—Charles Henry, drowned in childhood.

OBSERVATIONS.

Mr. John Dabney was a distinguished lawyer, and a Judge of
the Circuit Court of Virginia; he lived in Campbell County. In
1804 he was elected to the Senate of Virginia, and died in 1814.
His son, George Edward, was a Professor in Washington College
many years, and afterwards in Richmond College, until the commencement of the Civil War. He died March, 1868, just one
month before his brother, leaving no children.

Sketch of Mr. John Dabney, taken from the Records of his
son, the Rev. John Blair Dabney:

"John Dabney was the second son of Captain George Dabney,
and at an early age, applied himself to the study of law, and for
this purpose he resided for some time with his relative, Judge
Winston. About the year 1804–5, he was elected to the Senate
of Virginia, where he served the regular term of four years. Of
political life he soon became weary, for it was uncongenial to his
nature, and as soon as the period for which he was elected expired,
he returned with delight to the bosom of his family and his habitual
pursuits. In politics he had embraced, from sincere convictions,
the opinions of his father. He loved his country, and he loved liberty. When therefore he espoused the creed of this political party
it was because he honestly believed that the principles and meas-
ures of that party were conducive to the prosperity of his country.

After retiring from the Senate he continued to pursue his profession with undiminished industry and success, until the year 1813, when Judge Winston, his old friend and patron, having resigned his Judicial office, he was appointed, by a decided majority of the Legislature, to fill the vacant seat on the bench. This appointment gave general satisfaction in the Circuit, and during the despatch of business, his impartiality, his dignified amenity of manners, his promptitude of decision, his legal learning, his firmness and independence were acknowledged and applauded even by those who were originally hostile to his promotion. He died May 4th, 1814, in the prime of life."

RECORD NO. 56

(Given by John Dabney, of Salem, Roanoke County, Virginia.)

John Blair Dabney, son of John Dabney and Susanna Morris, and his wife, Elizabeth Lewis Towles.

SEVENTH GENERATION.

First.—John, born in 1822. Married Miss Lavinia Langhorne, of Botetourt County, Virginia. Living at date (1886) in Salem, Roanoke County, Virginia.

Mr. John Dabney died in Greenville, Mississippi, November 25th, 1887.

Second.—Maria Louisa, born in 1825. Married William C. Carrington, in 1848, who died in 1851. Living at date in Richmond, 1887.

Third.—Susan Morris, born in 1827. Married Edmund Taylor, of Caroline County, in 1845. Living at date of Blair Records, a widow.

Fourth.—Belle Lewis, born in 1829. Married Peter Saunders. Living at date, as is her husband (1887).

Fifth.—William Oliver, born in 1832. Died at College in 1850.

Sixth.—Charles Edward, lawyer, unmarried, and living (1887.) He graduated at Washington and the University of Virginia, and was a cavalry officer during the Civil War. He lives in Franklin County, Virginia.

Seventh.—Catherine Morris married Charles Preston, of Smythe County, Virginia, his second wife. Died in 1881, leaving one son, John Blair Preston.

Eighth.—Caroline Agatha, born in 1841, died about 1865, unmarried. Much lamented, as she was very lovely.

Ninth.—Chiswell, born in 1844. Married Miss Lucy Dabney Fontaine.

OBSERVATIONS.

Sketch of John Blair Dabney, written by his son, John Dabney, of Salem, Roanoke County, Virginia.

"John Blair Dabney, the son of John Dabney and Susanna Morris, was born in November of 1795. He was named for Parson Blair, with whom his father was on terms of the most intimate and affectionate friendship. He showed very early indications of remarkable capacity, which were carefully fostered and developed by his parents, and the best teachers were called into requisition for his instruction, and being studious beyond his years, when boys are usually digging into the rudiments of knowledge, he was prepared to enter college. He was sent to Hampden Sydney College, where he was remarkable for his assiduous devotion to his studies and irreproachable conduct. After completing his studies at this college he was sent to Princeton College, which then enjoyed the highest reputation of any college in the United States. On graduating he received the first honors of his class, and although commencement speeches are generally ephemeral and frothy in their character, and filled with youthful crudities, yet I have been informed that passages from his 'On the Partition of Poland,' are still selected as fine specimens of oratorical excellence, for purposes of declamation in that institution. After his return from Princeton, he applied himself to the study of law, and in due time received his license, and embarked in that profession.

Although not wealthy, he was in comfortable circumstances, and did not devote himself exclusively to his profession, but also to his farm, and to literary labors. He wrote much for the *Southern Literary Messenger*, which gained him a high reputation in literary circles as an elegant and accomplished writer.

"He possessed a highly cultivated mind, and had traversed the whole range of ancient and modern literature, and had so digested and arranged them in his mind that they were always ready to respond to the call of memory. In composition his style was smooth and elegant. By invitation he delivered addresses before the literary societies of Washington College, and William and Mary's College; and the latter institution conferred upon him the degree of L. L. D. From youth to age Judge William Leigh, Judge John Robertson, Bishop Johns and many others were his confidential and intimate friends. He married at the age of twenty-seven years Elizabeth Lewis Towles, a daughter of Major Oliver Towles, of Lynchburg, Virginia, and grand-daughter of Colonel Oliver Towles, an officer who fought with distinction in the Revolution through the whole of the war, and was wounded and taken prisoner at the battle of Germantown. Her mother was Agatha Lewis, a member of that Lewis family which bore so conspicuous a part in the settlement and early history of Western Virginia. She was a daughter of William Lewis, a brother of General Andrew Lewis, who commanded at the Battle of Point Pleasant, and of Colonel Charles Lewis, who was killed in the same battle. "Vaucluse" was the name of J. Blair Dabney's residence, which was the centre of generous hospitality, and from spring to autumn was crowded with visitors. Some twelve years before his death he entered the ministry of the Episcopal Church, and the latter part of his life he spent in zealous and conscientious attention to his duties as Rector of Moore Parish, Campbell County, Virginia. His death, which occurred in April, 1868, although sudden, did not find him unprepared."

CHART OF JOHN BLAIR DABNEY'S DESCENDANTS.

6th Generation.	*7th Generation.*

John Blair Dabney.

1. John Dabney.

2. Maria Louisa Dabney.

3. Susan Morris Dabney.

4. Belle Lewis Dabney.

5. Charles Edward Dabney.

6. Catherine Morris Dabney.

7. William Oliver Dabney.

8. Caroline Agatha Dabney.

9. Chiswell Dabney.

Elizabeth Lewis Towles.

No. on Chart.	Index.	No. Gen.	No. Record
	John Blair Dabney and Elizabeth Lewis Towles..............................	7	56
1	John Dabney and Lavinia A. Langhorne...	8	57
2	Maria Louisa Dabney and Wm. C. Carrington......................	8	58
3	Susan Morris Dabney and Edmund Taylor	8	59
4	Belle Lewis Dabney and Peter Saunders...	8	60
9	Chiswell Dabney and Lucy Dabney Fontaine	8	61

RECORD NO. 57

(Given by John Dabney, of Salem, corrected by W. H. Dabney.)

John Dabney, son of John Blair Dabney and Elizabeth Lewis Towles, and his wife, Lavinia A. Langhorne.

EIGHTH GENERATION.

First.—William L. married Miss Eliza Wietbury, and lives in Chicago, Illinois, and has two children.

Second.—Elizabeth Lewis went as a missionary to Africa, and married Rev. John McNabb, also a missionary there. They now reside in Accomac County, Virginia.

Third.—John Blair married Miss Lola Blanton, of Mississippi, and is living at date in Mississippi, and has two children.

Fourth.—Kate Montgomery living, unmarried.

Fifth.—Maria Carrington living, unmarried.

OBSERVATIONS.

Mr. John Dabney has just died at the age of sixty-five years, at the residence of his son, Mr. Blair Dabney, in Greenville, Mississippi. He had been in declining health for the last two years; last winter he spent with his daughter, Mrs. McNabb, in Accomac, Virginia, where he improved somewhat, and the last summer he passed in the mountains of Virginia in the summer home of his niece, Mrs. R. A. Lancaster, but he did not there improve as was expected and hoped. In the early autumn he returned to his old home in Salem, Virginia, which he sold, and then went to pass the winter with his son, Blair Dabney, in Greenville, Mississippi, but the long journey proved too much for his weakened frame, and he declined rapidly after reaching that place, and died there on the 25th of November, 1887.

He was born in 1822, and was educated at Washington College, and was a teacher and a professor for many years. He was a man of fine literary attainments, warm in his attachments, and with a heart overflowing with the milk of human kindness. Of him

H

Judge William Pope Dabney says: "He was an elegant gentle-man, and had all the distinctive features of the Dabneys."

From an obituary of him, I make the following extract: "Professor Dabney was about sixty-six years of age, and was the embodiment of those manly virtues, truth and honesty. He was a faithful member of the Episcopal Church, and to his untiring zeal and energy in its behalf, is due, to a very great extent, the hand-some improvements recently made to St. John's Church in this place. While that stone structure stands his memory will live, and of him it can truly be said that the world was better for his having lived in it. Peace be to the ashes of this good old man."

Mr. Dabney served throughout the Civil War as a private in the ranks.

RECORD NO. 58

(Given by John Dabney, of Salem, Virginia.)

William C. Carrington and Maria Louisa Dabney, daughter of John Blair Dabney and Elizabeth Lewis Towles.

EIGHTH GENERATION.

First.—Bessie Lewis married James N. Dunlop, member of the Virginia House of Legislature, and has five children.

Second.—Williamine married Robert A. Lancaster, of Rich-mond, Virginia.

OBSERVATIONS.

Mr. Carrington was a noted journalist of Richmond, Virginia, and died in 1851, three years after marriage. Mrs. Carrington is living at date (1887), and resides in Richmond with her son-in-law, R. A. Lancaster.

RECORD NO. 59

(J. Blair Dabney Records.)

Edmund Taylor and Susan Morris Dabney, daughter of John Blair Dabney and Elizabeth Lewis Towles.

EIGHTH GENERATION.

First.—Blair Dabney, surgeon in the United States army, married Miss Mary Allen, and has three children.

Second.—Lucy W. married Charles Preston, of Smythe County, Virginia, and was his third wife.

Third.—Ann Montgomery married James C. Langhorne; has three children, and lives in Colorado.

Fourth.—Bessie L. living, unmarried.

Fifth.—Edward, residence unknown.

Sixth.—William O.

Seventh.—Carrie M. married William Gold.

Eighth.—Agatha married David Walker, of Lynchburg, Virginia, and has one child.

Ninth.—Susan Taylor living, unmarried.

OBSERVATIONS.

Mr. Taylor was from Caroline County, Virginia, and is dead. Mrs. Taylor was living, a widow, with her children in 1880.

RECORD NO. 60

(J. Blair Dabney Records.)

Peter Saunders and Belle Lewis Dabney, daughter of John Blair Dabney and Elizabeth Lewis Towles.

EIGHTH GENERATION.

First.—Edward.

Second.—Agatha.

Third.—William.

Fourth.—Alice Lee.

OBSERVATIONS.

Mr. Saunders and family are living on his estate called "Hunter's Hall," in Franklin County, Virginia. He has represented his county in the Virginia Legislature on several occasions, and was there in 1880.

RECORD NO. 61

(J. Blair Dabney Records.)

Chiswell Dabney, son of John Blair Dabney and Elizabeth Lewis Towles, and his wife, Miss Lucy Dabney Fontaine.

EIGHTH GENERATION.

First.—John Charles.

Second.—Chiswell.

Third.—Louise Shackleford.

Fourth.—Lucy Fontaine.

Fifth.—Edmund Fontaine.

OBSERVATIONS.

Chiswell Dabney was the ninth child of the Rev. John Blair Dabney, and was born in 1844. He entered the Confederate army at the outbreak of the Civil War, at the age of seventeen years. He was soon made a Lieutenant, and then a Captain of Cavalry, and was at one time Aide de Camp to General Stuart. He married in 1873, and now resides in Chatham, Pittsylvania County, Virginia, where he is an attorney-at-law.

Mrs. Dabney was a daughter of Colonel E. Fontaine, of Hanover County, Virginia.

RECORD NO. 62

(Taken from the J. Blair Dabney Records.)

Lynn Shackleford and Elizabeth Dabney, eighth child of Captain George Dabney and Miss Elizabeth Price.

FIFTH GENERATION.

First.—Louisa Shackleford married Colonel Edmund Fontaine, of Hanover County, and left at her death a large family of children.

Mrs. Shackleford married again William Pollard, of Hanover County. They had one son.

Second.—George William married Miss Todd, his cousin, and lived in Hanover.

Mrs. Elizabeth Dabney Pollard was a very lovely woman, both in person and character.

RECORD NO. 63

(J. Blair Dabney Records.)

Chiswell Dabney, the eleventh child and youngest of Captain George Dabney and Miss Elizabeth Price, and his wife, Miss Norvell.

First.—George William died, unmarried.

Second.—Elizabeth married Major John S. Langhorne, of Lynchburg, Virginia, deceased, leaving three children.

Third.—John died, unmarried.

Fourth.—Mary Jane died, unmarried.

Fifth.—Nancy died, unmarried.

Sixth.—Lucy married M. Van R. Otey, of Lynchburg, Virginia, and left three children.

Seventh.—Catherine married Dr. Thomas L. Walker, of Lynchburg, Virginia, and has several children; she was the only one living in 1886.

Chiswell Dabney married a second time Miss Nancy Wyatt, and a third time Mrs. Elizabeth Lee, *nee* Tabb. Chiswell Dabney was named after Colonel Chiswell, who was a distant relative of the family. This gentleman was of English origin, and came from somewhere near Portland, England, in which part there is a village named Chiswell. He was a distinguished, but very eccentric man.

In Sketches and Recollections of Lynchburg, Virginia, we find under date of 1858, a notice of Chiswell Dabney and wife, which states:

" That he was a native of the County of Hanover. About the year 1812 he settled in Lynchburg, and commenced the practice of law. He has continued to add constantly to his legal reputation since that time, and to secure the regards and esteem of the community in which he resides. His talents as a lawyer, and his ability as an efficient bank officer, are too well known to need any eulogy, but it is a great gratification to associate the name of this gentleman with that of Mrs. Nancy Dabney, his wife, who was the oldest daughter of Thomas Wyatt, Esq. This lady was a native of Amherst, where were spent her childhood and youth, but she was educated in Lynchburg, and our town naturally feels desirous to claim as one of its own daughters, this bright, talented and excellent lady. She was a very superior woman, endowed with a mind of the highest order, and gifted with wit most brilliant, though ever tempered with gentleness and good humor. This excellent lady died in the summer of 1824, leaving five daughters, at that time a lovely and unbroken household. About 1842 two of these daughters were called hence to join their mother, a week only intervening between their deaths. Three survive, viz.: Mrs. John S. Langhorne, of Amherst; Mrs. Lucy Otey, of Campbell, and Mrs. Dr. Walker, of Lynchburg." Mr. Chiswell Dabney died in 1865.

RECORD NO. 64

(Supplied by John Dabney, of Salem, Virginia.)

John S. Langhorne and Elizabeth Dabney, daughter of Chiswell Dabney and Miss Norvell.

SEVENTH GENERATION.

First.—Chiswell Dabney married Miss Keene, of Pittsylvania County, Virginia, and has several children; his oldest married Moncure Perkins, of Richmond, Virginia.

Second.—Ann married Edward Hutter, of Lynchburg, Virginia, and has children.

Third.—Elizabeth married John Lewis, a lawyer of Lynchburg, Virginia.

Fourth.—Lucy.

Fifth.—Thomas.

RECORD NO. 65

(From J. Blair Dabney Records.)

Charles Dabney, second son of Colonel William Dabney, of Aldringham, and his wife, Miss Barrett.

"Colonel Charles Dabney, the second son of Colonel William Dabney, was one of the most remarkable of men of his day. In his early youth he marched from Hanover in that gallant band, which in the commencement of our troubles, extorted from the reluctant Dunmore, the surrender of the public powder, which that arbitrary governor had removed from the magazine at Williamsburg, with the view of depriving the insurgent colonists of the means of resisting his tyranny.

" The same patriotic enthusiasm which prompted Colonel Dabney to engage in the enterprise I have just alluded to, impelled him soon afterwards into our Revolutionary struggle. He was appointed a captain in the Virginia line soon after the commencement of the war, and was ultimately promoted to the rank of Colonel in the same service. After remaining with his command one or two years in his native state, where to his great chagrin, no military operations imposed upon him any active service, he was transferred to the Northern army shortly before the Battle of Monmouth. He was present at that undecisive action, and I have frequently heard him mention the extreme heat of that day, in consequence of which he saw many expiring on the field from mere exhaustion, and without a wound.

" In the preliminary arrangement of the American forces he was attached to that part of our army commanded by General Smallwood, and he bore the most decided testimony to the coolness and undaunted courage of that gallant and meritorious officer. Smallwood's ordinary demeanor, according to his account, was calm and quiet, and the only change which could be perceived in that gentleman's bearing on the eve of battle, was an increased degree of animation. Colonel Dabney fully sustained, from his own recollection of that battle, and of the statements of his brother officers, the charge of misconduct and disobedience of orders, of which General Lee was subsequently convicted by the sentence of a court martial. Whether that officer acted treacherously on that occasion, he did not undertake to determine, but he was decidedly of opinion that Lee was an ambitious, disappointed man, impatient at all times of subordination, and particularly chagrined that Washington, his inferior, as his vanity suggested, in military fame and experience, should have been elevated to the chief command of the American forces, in preference to himself.

With such feelings he could not have been expected to enter very heartily into the execution of any plan calculated to promote the glory of a man who had supplanted him in the darling objects of his life.

"Colonel Dabney continued to share the fortunes of the Northern army until that glorious consummation of their trials, the capitulation of Yorktown. He took part under the command of General Wayne, in that brilliant exploit, the Storming of Stony Point, one of the most daring and hazardous enterprises undertaken during the war. Colonel Dabney entertained no very exalted opinion of the military or personal character of General Putnam, nor was this the result of prejudice, for he always admitted the General's courage to be unquestionable, and with regard to the General's son, Major Putnam, he bore willing testimony to his high qualifications as an officer. Colonel Dabney's services ended with the Siege of Yorktown, in which he bore a conspicuous part.

"Though he took a lively interest in public affairs, and had very decided opinions, politically, he was never known to seek advancement, either at the hands of the people or the government, and scrupulously shunned the brawls, the intrigues, and the debasing scenes which disgraced our popular elections. He was prompt to obey the call of duty in the crisis of his country's peril, but he never coveted distinction in the halcyon days of peace. He disdained to court public favor, either for the gratification of personal vanity, or the promotion of his private interests. The only popularity which he valued, to use the noble language of Lord Mansfield, 'was that which follows, not that which is run after,' and this popularity he obtained, if ever man did. Unambitious, possessed of an independent fortune, and without any family of his own—for he was never married—he found in the tranquil pursuits, and simple pleasures of private life, sufficient exercise for his faculties, and an ample fund of happiness.

"Prior to the Revolution the means of intellectual cultivation were scanty in this country, and none of our citizens, except those whose abundant resources enabled them to visit the literary institutions of the old world, could aspire to the reputation of finished scholars. In point of education, my uncle, like most of his cotemporaries, enjoyed very moderate advantages, but his natural understanding was excellent, and he enriched his mind with a large stock of valuable knowledge, derived from his own observation, and intercourse with intelligent men. His opinions on all subjects indicated sound, practical sense, and as his moral perceptions were unperverted by any vicious habit, his judgments in matters of conscience were rarely erroneous, hence he was frequently consulted as an impartial and enlightened adviser on questions of right and expediency, not only by his own relations, but by his acquaintances generally. His councils were always freely and kindly given, and uniformly pointed to the path of duty and honor. Those who acted on his instructions, never had any reason to repent compliance therewith, for they were equally prudent and sagacious, evincing alike upright principles, and a thorough knowledge of human nature.

" That Colonel Dabney's natural capacity was of a high order, and would have made him conspicuons in any sphere where he chose to exert it, must have been obvious to all who had the pleasure of his acquaintance, but I prefer to dwell upon those moral excellencies, those admirable qualities of heart and disposition, which reflect the brightest and purest lustre on his well spent life. He was the most generous and charitable of men; in his personal habits he was economical, almost to parsimony, but this extreme frugality was practiced by him on principle, and not from any love of filthy lucre. He saved that he might have wherewithal to give, and I hazard little in affirming that during his long life, he gave away more money than any man in Virginia of much larger resources. His brothers, sisters, nephews and nieces were the constant subjects of his liberality, and he annually supplied many of his poor neighbors with the necessaries of life, but there

was nothing ostentatious in this perennial stream of benevolence;
so far from vaunting his good deeds, he was never known to allude
to them. On the scriptural principle, he gave in secret, believing
—for he was a sincere and consistent Christian—that 'His Father
in Heaven who seeth in secret, would reward him openly." His
benefactions were not only hidden from the public eye, but were
administered with the most refined delicacy, so that they might
produce no painful mortification in the effects of his bounty.

"No man was ever more sincerely and unaffectedly pious than
Colonel Dabney; his religion, while it pervaded his whole life
and conversation, had no tincture of sourness or austerity. Though
an Episcopalian from education and early predilections, his
Catholic spirit embraced in the circle of brotherly love, every
denomination of sincere Christians. He was careless about forms,
where he found the essentials of religion, and no word of censure
or derision was ever heard to pass his lips to the prejudice of any
association of devout men, who held their faith in the purity of
life; yet for cant, hypocrisy, or bigotry wherever manifested, he
had no toleration. In his devotions he was uniformly regular,
without being obtrusive; he made no ostentatious parade of his
piety, although it breathed unconsciously in every act of his life,
and diffused an odor of sanctity, a celestial benignity through his
whole character. Such is the faint outline of his moral qualities.
In stature he was upwards of six feet, with a body straight and
athletic, and well proportioned. His carriage was dignified and
commanding, and his gait slow and measured, like that of a soldier
on parade, a remnant of his old military habits. Accustomed
from his youth to active pursuits and violent exercise, inured to
hardship and exposure by the rough trade of war, and by hunting,
to which he was passionately addicted, temperate and regular in
his habits, his physical powers attained uncommon vigor, and
secured to his declining years a remarkable exemption from the
infirmities of old age. His visage was massive and well defined,
with a serene expression, betokening sound sense, firmness and

benevolence. There was something in his whole appearance and demeanor which deterred the most thoughtless and audacious from venturing upon too familiar an approach to so imposing a personage, and yet his deportment was so hearty, and cordial, and unaffected, that no one, young or old, felt any disagreeable constraint in his presence; he had the knack of putting every one at their ease, by an unstudied, unceremonious politeness, which was but the type and outward reflection of the heart; indeed I have never met with any one who had, in so eminent a degree, the faculty of making himself an agreeable companion to every description of person. He died about the year 1830, at the advanced age of eighty-five years, at his house in the County of Hanover, in which his father had lived."

This house remained in possession of the Dabney family until 1885, when it was sold.

In the collection of papers in the State Library of Virginia, entitled "Calendar of State Papers," Colonel Charles Dabney figures largely.

RECORD NO. 66
(Taken from the J. Blair Dabney Records.)

Samuel Dabney, third son of William Dabney, of Aldringham, and Miss Barrett, and his wife, Miss Merriwether.

FIFTH GENERATION.

First.—Thomas went to Pennsylvania, and there married a Dutch girl; had one son, Lewis, who married and had children.

Second.—Dr. Samuel settled as a physician in Caswell County, North Carolina, and there married a lady of fortune. Later he represented his county in the State Legislature in 1812, and then removed to Clarksville, Tennessee, and there died, leaving a numerous family.

Third.—Charles married Miss Price, daughter of Captain Samuel Price.

Fourth.—Francis was a lawyer, and never married.

Fifth.—William married Miss Hall, but left no children.

Sixth.—Richard, a poet and a man of genius; he never married.

Seventh.—Robert died, unmarried.

Eighth.—Edmund died in a lunatic asylum.

Ninth.—George was an officer in the War of 1812, and died unmarried.

Tenth.—John went to Tennessee, and there married, but it is not known if he left children.

Eleventh.—Elizabeth died, unmarried; she was an exemplary and noble woman, and devoted herself to her brother Edmund.

Twelfth.—Mildred married Mr. Lewis, brother of Merriwether Lewis. They had no children.

Thirteenth.—Mary Jane died in childhood.

OBSERVATIONS.

Samuel Dabney resided in Louisa County, Virginia. His wife, Miss Merriwether, of Albemarle County, Virginia, was an aunt of Merriwether Lewis, who, in conjunction with Colonel Clark, conducted their celebrated expedition to the mouth of the Columbia River in the years 1804 to 1806.

Mr. Dabney died while his children were very young, and as his estate was not large, his widow, who survived him for many years, had great difficulty in maintaining and educating her young and numerous family, and was much assisted in this by her brother-in-law, Colonel Charles Dabney. Charles Dabney, her son, assisted his uncle in the management of his estate, and at his death inherited it from him.

In "Duyckink's Cyclopædia of American Literature," is the following notice of Richard Dabney, son of Samuel:

"Richard Dabney was born about 1787, in Louisa County, Virginia, of a family settled for several generations in that State, which, in early times in England, had been Daubeney, and earlier still is said to have been D'Aubigny or D'Aubigné, of France. Richard's instruction was of the plainest rudiments of knowledge until his sixteenth or eighteenth year, when he went to a school of Latin and Greek. In these languages he strode forward with great rapidity, learning in one or two years more than most boys learn in six. He was afterwards assistant teacher in a Richmond school. From the burning theater of that city, in December of 1811, he barely escaped with life, receiving injuries which he bore with him to the grave. In 1812 he published a 12mo. volume of poems, and was said to have written a large part of 'Cary's Olive Branch.' In a few years he returned to his native place, where his widowed mother with some children lived upon her farm. Here he spent the remainder of his life in devouring such books and pamphlets as he could find, and visiting the neighboring farmers. He had contracted the habit of opium eating, and this with other excesses, brought him to his end in November 25, 1825, at the age of thirty-eight years. He died unmarried. His prevailing traits of mind were memory and imagination; his excellence was only in literature, for mathematics and the sciences he had no taste."

CHART OF SAMUEL DABNEY'S DESCENDANTS.

4th Generation.	*5th Generation.*
1. Samuel Dabney.	
	2. Thomas Dabney.
	3. Samuel Dabney.
	4. Charles Dabney.
	5. Francis Dabney.
	6. William Dabney.
	7. Richard Dabney.
	8. Robert Dabney.
	9. Edmund Dabney.
	10. George Dabney.
	11. John Dabney.
	12. Elizabeth Dabney.
	13. Mildred Dabney.
Miss Merriwether.	

No. on Chart.	Index.	No. Gen.	No. Record.
1	Samuel Dabney and Miss Merriwether....	4	66
3	Samuel Dabney 2nd and first and second wives..........................	5	67
4	Charles Dabney and Elizabeth Price......	5	68
6	William Dabney.........................	5	69
	Charles Wm. Dabney and Cordelia Watson	6	
	Rev. Robt. L. Dabney and Frances Morrison	6	70
	George Francis Dabney and Louisa Dabney	6	72

RECORD NO. 67

(Given by Rev. R. L. Dabney.)

Dr. Samuel Dabney, son of Samuel Dabney, of Cub Creek, Virginia, and Jane Merriwether, and his first wife, Miss Hobson, of Caswell County, North Carolina.

SIXTH GENERATION.

First.—Samuel, Jr., a physician, married Miss Minor, and left children.

Second.—Daughter married Mr. Rivers, of Kentucky, and is living (1887) in Paducah, Kentucky.

Third.—Daughter married Mr. Rivers, brother of her sister's husband.

After the death of his young wife, Dr. Samuel Dabney moved to Tennessee, and settled in Montgomery County, eight miles from Clarksville, and there married a second time Jane Harrison. Their children were:

SIXTH GENERATION.

First.—Lucy married Mr. Smith, of Clarksville, Tenn., and is living there (1887) a widow with two daughters, Margaret and Anna.

Second.—Margaret married Mr. Calvin F. Vance, of Memphis, Tennessee, and is living there (1887). They had three children; Lucy married Mr. Gregory, who is now dead, and a son Frank and daughter Bessie living. (Lucy and Margaret were twins).

Third.—Edmund is a physician in Ringold, Tennessee; is living and has several children.

Fourth.—Louisa married her cousin, George Francis Dabney, and is living in De Soto, Mississippi.

RECORD NO. 68

(J. Blair Dabney Records.)

Charles Dabney, son of Samuel Dabney and Miss Merriwether, and his wife, Miss Elizabeth Price.

SIXTH GENERATION.

First.—Charles William married Miss Cordelia Watson, and is living at date (1887) near Hanover Junction, Virginia.

Second.—Mary Jane married Mr. Johnson; living, a widow at date (1887).

Third.—Ann Eliza married Mr. Payne; living at date (1887) a widow.

Fourth.—Thomas Price died in infancy.

Fifth.—Barbara Winston died, unmarried.

Sixth.—Robert Lewis (Rev.) married Miss Frances Morrison, of Rockbridge County, living at date at Austin, Texas.

Seventh.—George Francis married his cousin, Miss Louisa Dabney, daughter of Dr. Samuel Dabney, Clarksville, Tennessee; living (1887) in De Soto City, Mississippi.

Eighth.—Elizabeth Catherine died, unmarried.

OBSERVATIONS.

Much confusion to those not knowing the fact exists in regard to Charles William and George Francis, as they have both dropped their first name, and are known among their friends as William and Francis.

Mr. John Blair Dabney says, speaking of Charles Dabney: " He resided many years with his uncle, Charles (Colonel Charles Dabney) assisting him in the management of his estates. When he married Miss Elizabeth Price he left his uncle's house, but Colonel Charles Dabney at his death made him his residuary legatee, and this proved a fortune to him. No man was ever more worthy of the gifts of fortune, for he had excellent sense and most amiable manners, was irreproachable in all relations of life, and of unquestionable integrity. Possessed of such sterling qualities of mind and heart, he was the idol of his own family, and universally respected by all his acquaintances. He was indeed a worthy successor to his most excellent uncle." He died some years after his benefactor, leaving a numerous and promising family. His eldest son, Charles William Dabney is now the owner and occupant of Colonel Charles Dabney's old homestead.

I am told this homestead was sold by the Dabney family about the year 1885.—F. D.

RECORD NO. 69

(Supplied by Dr. Charles William Dabney, Jr., of Raleigh, North Carolina.)

Charles William Dabney, son of Charles Dabney and Elizabeth Price, and his wife, Miss Cordelia Watson.

SEVENTH GENERATION.

First.—Charles is a farmer.

Second.—John Watkins married Miss Kate Gregory, and lives a missionary in Jundiahi, Province of Sao Paulo, Brazil, and has a family.

Third.—George, a railroad man, living in Minnesota.

Fourth.—Elizabeth Price living, unmarried (1887).

OBSERVATIONS.

Charles William Dabney resides in the old homestead of his father, near to Dalton Junction, Hanover County, Virginia. John Watkins Dabney married Miss Kate Gregory, daughter of Thomas Gregory and Sarah Day Nelson, whose mother was Susan Dandridge Dabney, daughter of George Dabney, of Dabney's Ferry. (See Record No. 11).

RECORD NO. 70

(Supplied by Dr. Charles William Dabney, Jr., of Raleigh, North Carolina.)

Rev. Robert L. Dabney, son of Charles Dabney and Elizabeth Price, and his wife, Miss Margaret Lavinia Morrison.

SEVENTH GENERATION.

First.—Dr. Charles William, Jr., born 1855; married Miss Mary Brant.

Second.—Samuel Brown, born 1857.

Third.—Lewis Merriwether, born in 1865.

I

OBSERVATIONS.

Mrs. Margaret Lavinia Morrison Dabney was from Rockbridge County, Virginia.

Rev. Robert L. Dabney is a well known divine in Virginia and elsewhere. During the war he was on the staff of General Stonewall Jackson, and after the war, wrote a life of this distinguished officer. He was for many years a Professor of Hampden Sydney College, and is now President of the University of Texas, and resides in Austin. He is the author of several theological works.

RECORD NO. 71

Charles William Dabney, Jr., son of Rev. Robert L. and Margaret L. M. Dabney, and his wife, Mary Brant.

EIGHTH GENERATION.

First.—Margarite Louise.

Second.—Mary Moore.

OBSERVATIONS.

Charles William Dabney, Jr., son of Rev. Robert L. Dabney, after studying and taking his degree of Ph. D. abroad, returned to Virginia, and was soon after appointed Director of the Agricultural Experimental Station of Raleigh, North Carolina, and resided there for some years; lately he has been chosen the President of the University of Tennessee, and resides in Knoxville.

RECORD NO. 72

(Supplied by Dr. Charles William Dabney, Jr., of Raleigh, North Carolina.)

George Francis Dabney, son of Charles Dabney and Elizabeth Price, and his wife, Miss Louisa Dabney (his cousin), daughter of Dr. Samuel Dabney, of Clarksville, Tennessee.

SEVENTH GENERATION.

First.—Francis, Jr., living (1887), unmarried.

Second.—Robert Lewis married Miss Caruther; living (1887), and has two children.

Third.—George.

Fourth.—Edmund died, unmarried.

Fifth.—Jane Gilmer, who is dead.

OBSERVATIONS.

Mr. George Francis Dabney resides in De Soto County, Mississippi, with his family.

RECORD NO. 73

(Supplied by Miss M. Emmilly Dabney.)

Robin Dabney, youngest son of Colonel William Dabney, of Aldringham, and Miss Barrett, and his wife, Barbara Winston.

FIFTH GENERATION.

First.—Joseph Ferrell married Miss Rachael Burnett Dickinson.

Second.—Charles died very young.

Third.—Robert went South and married; the name of his wife is unknown.

Fourth.—William married Miss Jemima, daughter of John and Mary Goodwin Harris.

Fifth.—Nancy married Mr. David Allen, of Louisa County; they had one daughter and one son. Mr. Allen died, and she married a second time Edward Cason, and had two children.

Sixth.—Eliza married J. Walter Hillman, and had two daughters, Lizzie and Belle; Lizzie married Mr. Melvin, and had one daughter, Belle. Mr. Melvin died, and Lizzie married Mr. Evans. Belle Hillman married Mr. McGruder; had a son, Henry.

OBSERVATIONS.

Robin Dabney was a man of considerable talent, a wit and humorist. He lived in Hanover County, as did most of his brothers and sisters, and his descendants are scattered throughout Hanover and Louisa Counties, Virginia. (J. Blair Dabney Records.)

Miss M. Emmilly Dabney writes: " That he lived on a large plantation in Hanover County, known as ' Dabney's Mills,' on account of extensive merchant flouring mills which he built. They were widely known, but were burned to the ground by an incendiary. He was the owner of over 1,000 slaves, and immensely wealthy."

CHART OF ROBIN DABNEY'S DESCENDANTS.

4th Generation.	*5th Generation.*

1. Robin Dabney.

2. Joseph Ferrell Dabney.

3. Charles Dabney.

4. Robert Dabney.

5. William Dabney.

6. Nancy Dabney.

7. Eliza Dabney.

Barbara Winston.

No. on Chart.	Index.	No. Gen.	No. Record.
1	Robin Dabney and Barbara Winston......	4	73
2	Joseph Ferrell Dabney and Rachael Burnett Dickinson.............................	5	74
	Robert Clarence Dabney and Margaret Millian Browne...........................	7	75
	Charles Wm. Dabney and Bethe Durett ..	7	76
	Joseph Ferrell Dabney, Jr., and Maria Durett	7	77
5	William Dabney and Jemima Harris......	6	78
6	Nancy Dabney and David Allen...........	6	79

RECORD NO. 74

(Given by Miss M. E. Dabney.)

Joseph Ferrell Dabney, oldest son of Robin Dabney and Barbara Winston, and his wife, Miss Rachael Burnett Dickinson.

First.—William Festus married Miss Lewellyn, and died without issue in 1858.

Second.—Robert Clarence, born in Louisa County, March 4, 1822. Married Miss Margaret Millian Browne, at Liberty, Spottsylvania County, Virginia, November 12, 1850; died in 1875.

Third.—Charles William married Miss Bethe Durett; died in 1885.

Fourth.—Joseph Ferrell, Jr., married Miss Maria Durett, sister of his brother Charles' wife.

Fifth.—John Walter married Miss Mary B. Reddick, daughter of Judge Reddick, died without issue in 1862. Mrs. Dabney is also dead.

Sixth.—James Winston married Miss Ella Smith; had seven children, Louisa, William, Norton, Everett, Bowie, Laura and Edwin. They live near Guiney's Depot, Caroline County, Virginia.

Seventh.—Henry Clay married Miss Mary Cramer, but his wife died soon, leaving two children, viz.: Florence Burnett and Walter Ferrell; they live in Montclair, Essex County, New Jersey.

Eighth.—Richard Dickinson married Miss Bettie Tompkins, who died without issue. He married a second time Mrs. McCormick, and lives in Parkersburg, West Virginia.

Ninth.—Mary Montague married Benjamin Anderson. They have two daughters: Eddie, who married W. W. Burgess, and has one daughter, Lillian B., and Willhelmina Minor, who married Frank Dabney, and has one child, Mary Temple.

Tenth.—Eliza Burnett, who never married.

Eleventh.—Tomasia Bradshaw married J. Henry Noland, of Charleston, West Virginia. They have one daughter, Grace Burnett, and they live in Charleston.

OBSERVATIONS.

Joseph Ferrell Dabney died in 1845, and his wife, Mrs. Mary B. Dabney died in 1885.

RECORD NO. 75
(Given by Miss M. E. Dabney.)

Robert Clarence Dabney, second son of Joseph Ferrell Dabney and Rachael Burnett Dickinson, and Miss Margaret Millian Browne.

SEVENTH GENERATION.

First.—Robert Clarence, born in Spottsylvania County, Virginia, September 9, 1851; died July 21, 1856.

Second.—Raleigh Travers, born in Spottsylvania County, Virginia, May 15, 1854. Married Mrs. Gibson, of Memphis, Tennessee. They reside in Peoria, Illinois, and have no children.

Third.—Clare Morton, born in Spottsylvania County, Virginia, October 8th, 1855. Married William Ward Ashby in 1877. They have one daughter, named Annie.

Fourth.—Margarett Emmilly, born in Spottsylvania County, Virginia, July 12th, 1858. Living with her mother and sisters in Washington at date (1887).

Fifth.—Mary Eliza, born in Spottsylvania County, Virginia, January 30, 1860. Living in Washington, D. C.

Sixth.—Annie Burnett, born in Spottsylvania County, Virginia, November 10, 1861. Living in Washington, D. C.

OBSERVATIONS.

Mr. Robert Clarence Dabney was for thirty years clerk of the Court of Spottsylvania, Virginia, and died a short time after his re-election to office, on the 1st of May, 1875. Mrs. Dabney was the daughter of Captain John Cooke Browne, who served with distinction in the war of 1812. He was a nephew of Colonel Cooke, of Revolutionary memory and fame; was one of the descendants of Sir Walter Raleigh, and was related to General Washington through the Balls, of Virginia.

Captain John Cooke Browne married Miss Eliza Morton, of Maryland. She was a niece of Lieutenant Allen Waller, who was with General Wolfe at the storming of Quebec, and was killed in that battle. She was also a grand niece of Sir William Waller, the poet.

RECORD NO. 76
(Given by Miss M. E. Dabney.)

Charles William Dabney, third son of Joseph Ferrell Dabney and Rachael Burnett Dickinson, and Miss Bethe Durett.

SEVENTH GENERATION.

First.—Ella married Herbert Welton, and has one son, Walter Raymond.

Second.—Bessie, unmarried.

Third.—Mary married Mercer A. Nunn, and has one daughter named Ethel M.

Fourth.—Charles, unmarried.

Fifth.—Shepherd, unmarried.

Sixth.—Lillian, unmarried.

OBSERVATIONS.

Charles William Dabney is dead, and his widow resides with her children near Guiney's Depot, Caroline County, Virginia.

RECORD NO. 77
(Given by Miss M. E. Dabney.)

Joseph Ferrell Dabney, Jr., son of Joseph Ferrell Dabney and Rachael Burnett Dickinson, and Miss Maria Durett.

SEVENTH GENERATION.

First.—Mattie married Otho. Wigglesworth; they have two children, Percy and Bessie.

Second.—Frank married his cousin, Willie Anderson, and lives in Childsburg, Caroline County, Virginia.

Third.—Joseph Curtis died in infancy.

Fourth.—Joseph Ferrell 3d.

Fifth.—Lucy.

Sixth.—Ruth.

Seventh.—Eliza married William Hancock, December 22, 1887.

RECORD NO. 78
(Given by Miss M. E. Dabney.)

William Dabney, fourth son of Robin Dabney and Barbara Winston, and his wife, Jemima Harris.

SIXTH GENERATION.

First.—Mary married Dr. Pendleton.

Second.—Elizabeth married John Mercer Waller, who was the son of Sarah Dabney and Thomas Waller, and grandson of John Dabney, of Spottsylvania, and Anna Harris.

Third.—Maria married Mr. Perkins.

Fourth.—Martha married Reuben Sizer.

Fifth.—Fanny married Mr. Goodwin.

RECORD NO. 79
(Given by Miss M. K. Dabney.)

Nancy Dabney, oldest daughter of Robin Dabney and Barbara Winston, and David Allen.

SIXTH GENERATION.

First.—Ann married Harvey Sharp.   Their children are Robert, Annie, Harvey and Susie.

Second.—Alexander never married.

Mr. Allen died, and his widow married a second time Edward Cason. Their children were:

First.—Robert, who never married.

Second.—Bethe, who married Mr. Pierce.

RECORD NO. 80
(Taken from the J. Blair Records.)

William Morris and Elizabeth Dabney, daughter of William Dabney, of Aldringham, and Miss Barrett.

FIFTH GENERATION.

First.—William married Miss Watson, and died in 1831. He had ten children.

Second.—John moved to Frankfort, Kentucky, and there married Miss Innes. He lived to over eighty years of age.

Third.—Dr. Charles married Miss Emily Taylor, and had six children.

Fourth.—Richard married in 1809 Miss Mary Watts; died in 1831, and had seven children.

Fifth.—Catherine, who never married.

Sixth.—Ann married Colonel William Fontaine, and had eight children.

Seventh.—Susanna Dabney married John Dabney, her first cousin.

OBSERVATIONS.

Mrs. Elizabeth Dabney Morris died about 1820, in the house of her daughter, Ann (Mrs. Fontaine), with whom she had resided for many years. She was a most exemplary, amiable and lovely woman, beloved by all who knew her.

William Morris was a son of Sylvanus Morris and Catherine Brodie, a Scotch lady, and was a grandson of William Morris, the original emigrant to Virginia, who died in 1746.

RECORD NO. 81

(Taken from J. Blair Dabney Records.)

William Morris, son of William Morris and Elizabeth Dabney, and his wife, Miss Watson.

SIXTH GENERATION.

First.—Ann married James Maury Morris, and had children.

Second.—Dr. John married Miss Susanna Pleasants, daughter of Governor James Pleasants, and had several children.

Third.—Joseph never married.

Fourth.—Harriet married Mr. Michie; had one daughter, Sarah.

Fifth.—Ellen married first, Mr. Carr, of Albemarle County; second, Mr. Barker, of Kentucky; left no children.

Sixth.—Juliet married James Fontaine, her cousin, and had many children.

Seventh.—Susan married James Watson, her cousin, and had two children.

Eighth.—James was a graduate of the University of Virginia. Married Miss Smith, daughter of Marcellus Smith.

Ninth.—Mary married Dr. Minor.

Tenth.—Elizabeth married Thomas S. Watson, brother of her sister Susan's husband, and her cousin. Mary and Elizabeth were twins.

Third Branch

OF THE

Virginia Dabneys.

BEING THE DESCENDANTS OF CORNELIUS D'AUBIGNÉ AND HIS
SECOND WIFE, SARAH JENNINGS, OR JENNENS.

THIRD BRANCH OF SOUTHERN DABNEYS. THEY BEING THE
DESCENDANTS OF CORNELIUS D'AUBIGNÉ, OR DABNEY,
THE ORIGINAL SETTLER, AND SARAH JENNENS,
OR JENNINGS, HIS SECOND WIFE.

1st Generation.	*2d Generation.*
1. Cornelius d'Aubigné, or Dabney. Married in England. First Wife. Married in 1721, to Second Wife. Sarah Jennens.	George Dabney. 2. William Dabney. 3. John Dabney. 4. Cornelius Dabney 2d. 5. Mary Elizabeth Dabney. 6. Fannie Dabney. 7. Mary Dabney. 8. Anna Dabney. 9. Mrs. Mathew Brown. 10. Mrs. Wm. Johnson.

No. on Chart.	Index.	No. Gen.	No. Record.
1	Cornelius d'Aubigné and Sarah Jennings...	1	82
2	William Dabney and Philadelphia Guath-mey..................................	2	83
3	John Dabney and wife, name unknown.....	2	106
4	Cornelius Dabney and Lucy Winston......	2	40

OBSERVATIONS.

As has already been stated, Cornelius d'Aubigné, with his older brother John d'Aubigné, came over from England to Virginia early in the Eighteenth Century, and settled on the York River, near the Piping Tree Ferry, where the river now divides the Counties of King William and Hanover.

The two brothers must have been well on in life when they came over, with children grown up. It is stated that soon after coming over, Cornelius' wife died. She was an invalid when she came, and therefore brought with her, to assist her in her house-keeping cares (as she had no daughters), Sarah Jennens. Not long after her death Cornelius married for a second wife, this same Sarah Jennens.

According to a statement made by Charles William Dabney, of Dalton Junction, Hanover County, Virginia, this second marriage took place in 1721. He states: "That he remembers seeing a Court Record in Hanover Court House, unfortunately destroyed in the fire of 1865. In the first Minute Book of this Court House, at the beginning of the entries (when the County was cut off from New Kent) under the date of —— April, 1726, the fol-lowing entry: 'Ordered that it be recorded, that on the —— day of April, 1721, Cornelius Dabney, late of England, intermarried with Sarah Jennings or Jennens, also of England.' It is founded on this date that we place the coming over of the two brothers, d'Aubigné, to have occurred some time between the dates of 1715 and 1720. Cornelius appears to have had an only son named George, by his first wife, who must have reached man's estate ere coming over with his parents, as he was married, and already had children at the time of his father's second marriage (1721.) He had many descendants, the records of one branch of which, viz: from his son, William, have been collected by the late Rev. John Blair Dabney, who also wrote memoirs of some of the most noteworthy members of this branch. This exists only in manu-script, in the possession of his sons, and has never been printed.

Cornelius d'Aubigné and Sarah Jennens had nine children, three sons and six daughters, as stated in his will, a copy of which is in the possession of William Winston Dabney, of Enfield, King William County, Virginia. This will was recorded in the County Court House, of Hanover, February 17, 1765. In it he names his wife, Sarah, and his children William, John, and Cornelius (who died before he did) as he mentions that his part of the estate should be sold and the proceeds divided among his deceased son's children. He names his son-in-law, Harris (his wife being also dead) his daughters Mary Elizabeth Maupin, Fanny Maupin and Anna Thompson, and the husbands of two others, Brown and Johnson, and appointed John Dabney and Henry Terrell his executors. This will was dated October 25th, 1764.

It will thus be seen that he reached a very old age, for allowing him to have been ten years old when he fled from Nantes, say from France, at the Revocation of the Edict of Nantes (1685), this would make him ninety years of age at the time of his death.

It is supposed that the reason his son George, by his first wife, was not mentioned in his will, was because he had previously provided for him during his lifetime. He appears to have left much property, including large tracts of land in Spottsylvania County, Va.

In some old State papers it is stated that in the very early history of the Virginia Colony, the Colonial Council allowed one Cornelius Dabney a certain amount of money as Interpreter to the Pamunky Indians; no doubt that this Cornelius Dabney is meant.

RECORD NO. 82

(Supplied by William Winston Dabney.)

Cornelius d'Aubigné or Dabney, the original settler in Virginia, and Sarah Jennings or Jennens, his second wife. Their children were:

SECOND GENERATION.

First.—William married Philadelphia Guathmey.

Second.—Cornelius 2d married Lucy Winston, sister of William Winston, of Langaloo.

Third.—Mary married Charles Harris.

Fourth.—Mary Elizabeth married Mr. Maupin.

Fifth.—Fanny married another Maupin.

Sixth.—Anna married Mr. Thompson.

Seventh.—John.

There were two other daughters, names not known, who married, the one Matthew Brown, and the other William Johnson, who are named in Cornelius d'Aubigné's will.

OBSERVATIONS.

The two Maupins above mentioned, most likely brothers, were, from their names, probably French Huguenots also. The late Dr. Socrates Maupin, who was Dean of the Faculty of the University of Virginia, and was killed by being thrown out of a carriage, claimed kinship with the Dabneys, and it was probably in this way.

RECORD NO. 83

(Supplied by William Winston Dabney.)

William Dabney, first son of Cornelius and Sarah Jennens Dabney, and Philadelphia Guathmey. Their children were:

THIRD GENERATION.

First.—Isaac married Elizabeth ———.

Second.—Owen married Miss Anderson.

Third.—Cornelius married Miss Elizabeth Smith.

Fourth.—Richard married Diana Guathmey.

Fifth.—William married Sallie Guathmey.

Sixth.—Guathmey married Miss Mordecai.

Seventh.—Lucy married.

Eighth.—Sarah married.

Ninth.—Philadelphia married.

OBSERVATIONS.

Of the daughters, one married Captain Mordecai Booth, and another Colonel Humphrey Brooke. The name of Guathmey is pronounced in Virginia as if it were spelled Goffney.

CHART OF WILLIAM DABNEY (OLDEST SON OF CORNELIUS
AND SARAH JENNENS, OR JENNINGS DABNEY) AND
HIS CHILDREN.

2d Generation.	3d Generation.
William Dabney.	1. Isaac Dabney.
	2. Owen Dabney.
	3. Cornelius Dabney.
	4. Richard Dabney.
	5. Wm. Dabney, Jr.
	6. Guathmey Dabney.
	7. Lucy Dabney.
	8. Sarah Dabney.
	9. Philadelphia Dabney.
Philadelphia Guathmey.	

No, on Chart	Index	No. Gen.	No. Record.
1	Isaac Dabney and Elizabeth ——..........	3	84
2	Owen Dabney and Miss Anderson.........	3	91
3	Cornelius Dabney and Elizabeth Smith....	3	92
4	Richard Dabney and Diana Guathmey....	3	103
5	William Dabney, Jr., and Sarah Guathmey	3	104
6	Guathmey Dabney and Miss Mordecai....	3	105

J

RECORD NO. 84
(Given by William Winston Dabney.)

Isaac Dabney, oldest son of William and Philadelphia Dabney, and his wife, Ann Hill.   Their children were:

FOURTH GENERATION.

First.—William married Hannah Temple Dabney, daughter of Richard Dabney (cousins).

Second.—Humphrey married the widow Katherine Collins.

Third.—Isaac.

Fourth.—Robert.

Fifth.—Frances married Richard Dabney, son of Richard Dabney and Diana Guathmey.

These were all the children named in his will.

OBSERVATIONS.

The date of Isaac Dabney's will is 1784.

RECORD NO. 85
(Supplied by William Winston Dabney.)

William Dabney, son of Isaac Dabney, and Hannah Temple Dabney, his wife.   There were two children, viz.:

FIFTH GENERATION.

First.—Diana married her father's cousin, Cornelius Dabney, son of William Dabney.

Second.—Richard.

These were their only children.

OBSERVATIONS.

Hannah Temple Dabney, wife of William Dabney, was his cousin, being a daughter of his uncle, Richard Dabney.

RECORD NO. 86
(Given by A. Dabney Barnes.)

Humphrey Dabney, son of Isaac Dabney and Ann Hill, and his wife, widow Katherine Collins.

FIFTH GENERATION.

First.—Katherine married Judge John Prentiss, of Sussex, and had children.

Second.—Sarah married John Carter Page, son of Governor John Page, and had children.

Third.—Mary Ann never married.

Fourth.—Susan Hill married John E. Baber, and has children.

Fifth.—Albert Gallatin married Susan Hill Segar, daughter of Dr. John Segar and Mrs. Collins, *nce* Frances Dabney, daughter of Isaac Dabney, and half sister to Hon. Joseph Segar.

OBSERVATIONS.

Humphrey Dabney married the widow Katherine Collins. Mrs. Collins had a daughter by her first husband, named Jane Collins, who married William McCabe, and their son was the father of William Gordon McCabe, Head Master of the University School, Petersburg, and of his sister, Mrs. Alfred Shield.

Mrs. Sarah Dabney Page is yet living (1887) at the advanced age of ninety-two years, with her daughter, Mrs. Virginia Edwards, in Portsmouth, Virginia.

RECORD NO. 87
(Given by A. Dabney Barnes.)

Albert Gallatin Dabney, son of Humphrey Dabney and Katherine Collins, and his wife, Susan Hill Segar.

SIXTH GENERATION.

First.—Humphrey married Roberta Blanks, and has one son named Albert.

Second.—Emma unmarried.

Third.—Alberta unmarried.

Fourth.—John Collins married Florence Henry Millar, and has two sons, Millar and Frederick, and one daughter, Margaret.

Fifth.—David M. unmarried.

Sixth.—Susan Segar unmarried.

(And six others, probably died young).

OBSERVATIONS.

Albert G. Dabney was named after the celebrated Albert Gallatin, who was related to the family. He was a master machinist, of Lynchburg, and was widely known and highly esteemed. His widow is living (1887), in Lynchburg, Virginia.

RECORD NO. 88
(Given by A. Dabney Barnes.)

Frances Dabney, daughter of Isaac Dabney and Ann Hill, and Richard Dabney, son of Richard and Diana (Guathmey) Dabney. They had five children, of which only two grew up, viz.:

FIFTH GENERATION.

First.—Richard.

Second.—Catherine married John Hilliard, of King William County.

Mr. Dabney died, and Mrs. Dabney married Dr. John Segar, of King William County. They had five children, viz.:

First.—Susan Hill married Albert Gallatin Dabney, her cousin,.

Second.—Rebecca Ann married Joseph A. Barnes, and is the mother of Albert Dabney Barnes.

Third.—Sarah Frances married William Toler, of Henrico County; and two sons, who died in early childhood.

RECORD NO. 89
(Supplied by William Winston Dabney.)

Cornelius Dabney, son of William Dabney and Sallie Guathmey, and his wife and second cousin, Diana Dabney, grand-daughter of Isaac Dabney. Their children were:

FIFTH AND SIXTH GENERATIONS.

First.—William Winston married Miss Martha Ann Bosher. I do not know of any other children.

OBSERVATIONS.

Mr. William Winston Dabney is living at date (1887), at Enfield, King William County, Virginia.

RECORD NO. 90

(Furnished by William Winston Dabney.)

William Winsto Dabney, son of Cornelius and Diana Dabney, and his wife, Martha Ann Bosher. Their children were:

SEVENTH GENERATION.

First.—James Edward.

Second.—William Winston, Jr., deceased.

Third.—Williana Winston, deceased.

Fourth.—Cornelius married Miss Nicol, of New Orleans, and is dead—two children, Cornelius and Kate Nicols Dabney.

Fifth.—Alfred Bosher, deceased.

Sixth.—Henry L.

Seventh.—Hannah Temple.

Eighth.—Owen Guathmey, deceased.

Ninth.—John Guathmey.

Tenth.—Joseph.

OBSERVATIONS.

Mr. William Winston Dabney resides in Enfield, King William County, Virginia, and is in possession of a large collection of family records, including a copy of the will of Cornelius d'Aubigné or Dabney, the original settler, and also notes of Cornelius de Bonis, de Bony, or de Bany, and others named Dabney, who were in Virginia very many years before the date at which it is supposed that Cornelius d'Aubigné and his brother John came over to Virginia.

RECORD NO. 91

(Supplied by William Winston Dabney.)

Owen Dabney, second son of William and Philadelphia Dabney, and his wife, Miss Anderson. Their children were:

FOURTH GENERATION.

First.—Robert married widow Booth.

Second.—Owen married (name of wife unknown).

Third.—John *not* married.

Fourth.—Nancy married Mr. Phillips.

Fifth.—Lucy married Mr. Johnson, and moved to Goochland.

Sixth.—Mary married Mr. Dickinson.

Seventh.—Elizabeth married Mr. Johnson.

Eighth.—Virginia, if married, not known.

Ninth.—Philadelphia married Mr. Stuart.

RECORD NO. 92

(Supplied by William Winston Dabney.)

Cornelius Dabney (third son of William and Philadelphia Guathmey Dabney), and his wife, Elizabeth Smith.

FOURTH GENERATION.

First.—Isaac Winston married first, Hannah Miller; second, Sarah Chew; third, name not known.

Second.—William Spotswood married Miss Jackson.

Third.—Cornelius married Mary Catlett, and emigrated to Kentucky or Tennessee in 1830.

Fourth.—Albert Gallatin married Ann Eliza Catlett, sister to his brother Cornelius' wife, and emigrated to Kentucky in 1830.

Fifth.—Elizabeth married Mr. Stuart (Methodist clergyman.)

Sixth.—Martha married Mr. Cooper, a Methodist clergyman.

OBSERVATIONS.

Cornelius Dabney resided in Louisa County, Virginia. His son, Albert G., was named for the celebrated Albert Gallatin, who was related to the family.

CHART OF CORNELIUS DABNEY (THIRD SON OF WILLIAM AND
PHILADELPHIA DABNEY) AND ELIZABETH SMITH'S
DESCENDANTS.

3d Generation.	4th Generation.
Cornelius Dabney.	1. Isaac Winston Dabney.
	2. William Spotswood Dabney.
	3. Cornelius Dabney.
	4. Albert Gallatin Dabney.
	5. Elizabeth Dabney.
	6. Martha Dabney.
Elizabeth Smith.	

No. on Chart.	Index.	No. Gen.	No. Record.
1	Isaac Winston Dabney and Hannah Millar	4	93
2	William Spotswood Dabney and Miss Jackson	4	94
3	Cornelius Dabney and Mary Catlett	4	95
4	Albert Gallatin Dabney and Ann Eliza Catlett	4	96

RECORD NO. 93

(Supplied by Edwin Winston Dabney.)

Isaac Winston Dabney, oldest son of Cornelius Dabney and
Elizabeth Smith, and his first wife, Hannah Millar.

FIFTH GENERATION.

First.—Eliza married Henry Hughes.

Second.—Catherine married Albert Merriwether.

Third.—Dorothy Ann married Thomas Merriwether.

Fourth.—Hannah Guathmey married Edwin Winston Dabney, her cousin.

Fifth.—Martha Winston married Henry Hughes.

Sixth.—A son, who died young.

Mr. Isaac Winston Dabney married a second time Sarah Chew. Their children all died young, also his wife. He then married a third wife; *name not known.* Their children were:

FIFTH GENERATION.

First.——— Winston married Miss Hughes, and had children.

Second.—Albert.

Third.—Urath married Mr. Crabster, and had children.

OBSERVATIONS.

Mr. Edwin Winston, who gives the above information, does not mention the name of Isaac Winston Dabney's third wife, and he says, "I do not know anything about the children of Winston and Miss Hughes; and do not know what became of Albert."

RECORD NO. 94
(Supplied by Edward Winston Dabney, of Texas.)

William Spotswood Dabney, second son of Cornelius Dabney and Elizabeth Smith, and his wife, Miss Jackson.

FIFTH GENERATION.

First.—Robert, married and died, leaving one son named Walter.

Second.—Frederick married Miss Nichols. Lives in Louisa County, Virginia. Children, if any, unknown.

Third.—Smith.

Fourth.—Bruce.

Fifth.—Mary Lucy.

Sixth.—Virginia.

RECORD NO. 95

(Supplied by Edwin Winston Dabney.)

Cornelius Dabney, third son of Cornelius Dabney and Elizabeth Smith, and Mary Ann Catlett.

FIFTH GENERATION.

First.—Cornelius married Miss Wiley, and had a large family of children. Lived in Louisa County, Virginia.

Second.—Charles. Died young.

Third.—Ann Eliza married Wiley Jones. Living at date in Virginia.

Fourth.—Caroline married. Name of husband unknown. Living at date in Virginia (1887.)

RECORD NO. 96

(Given by Dr. Archie Smith Dabney, of Paducah, Kentucky, corrected by his uncle, Edwin Winston Dabney, of Kenneyville, Texas.)

Albert Gallatin Dabney, fourth son of Cornelius Dabney and Elizabeth Smith, and Miss Ann Eliza Catlett.

FIFTH GENERATION.

First.—Edwin Winston, born in 1821, married his cousin, Hannah Guathmey Dabney, daughter of Isaac Winston Dabney.

Second.—Thomas Catlett (Judge) married Miss Rumsey, only child of James D. and Annie Rumsey, *nee* Somers.

Third.—Albert Smith married Pamelia Middleton.

Fourth.—Cornelius Isaac married Miss Susan Garnett; moved to Texas in 1853; died 1882.

Fifth.—John Temple died in infancy.

Albert G. Dabney married a second time Miss Elizabeth Scates. Their children were:

FIFTH GENERATION.

First.—Ann Maria married Mr. Carr, and lives in Texas.

Second.—Elizabeth married Walter Lewis.

Third.—Juliette O. married first, Robert Merriwether; second,

Mr. Price. Is living at Auburn, Logan County, Kentucky, in 1887.

Fourth.—Walter Scates married Lucy Dickinson first; second, married Texana Bibb.

Fifth.—Joseph Whorton married Lucy Ann Bowles.

Sixth.—William Spotswood. Died unmarried.

Seventh.—Virginia Louisa married H. C. Switzer.

Eighth.—Robert Owen. Died unmarried.

CHART OF ALBERT GALLATIN DABNEY (FOURTH SON OF WIL-
LIAM DABNEY AND ELIZABETH SMITH) AND FIRST
WIFE, ANN ELIZA HARRIS, AND SECOND
WIFE, ELIZABETH SCATES.

4th Generation.	*5th Generation.*
Albert Gallatin Dabney.	
	1. Edwin Winston Dabney.
	2. Thomas Catlett Dabney.
	3. Albert Smith Dabney.
	4. Cornelius Isaac Dabney.
Ann Eliza Catlett.	5. John Temple Dabney.
	6. Ann Maria Dabney.
	7. Elizabeth Dabney.
	8. Juliette O. Dabney.
	9. Walter Scates Dabney.
	10. Joseph Whorton Dabney.
	11. Wm. Spotswood Dabney.
	12 Virginia Louisa Dabney.
	13. Robert Owen Dabney.
Elizabeth Scates.	

No. on Chart.	Index.	No. Gen.	No. Record.
1	Edwin Winston Dabney and Hannah Guathmey Dabney	6	97
2	Thomas Catlett Dabney and Miss Rumsey	6	98
3	Albert Smith Dabney and Pamelia Middleton	6	99
4	Cornelius Isaac and Miss Susan Garnett	6	100
10	Joseph Whorton Dabney and Lucy Ann Bowles	6	102
9	Walter Scates Dabney and Lucy Dickinson Dabney	6	101

RECORD NO. 97

(Supplied by Edwin Winston Dabney.)

Edwin Winston Dabney, oldest son of Albert Gallatin Dabney and Ann Eliza Catlett, and his wife Hannah Guathmey Dabney, cousins.

SIXTH GENERATION.

First.—Ann Eliza married William Starks, and died young, leaving a son and daughter.

Second.—Albert Gallatin died young.

Third.—Hannah Elizabeth married Mr. Cox, and had *no* children.

Fourth.—Edwin married Miss Dickinson, and has five children, viz.: Edwin W., Allen D., Lucy, Nettie and Hannah.

Fifth.—Thomas.

Sixth.—Emma Juliet.

Seventh.—Cornelius Isaac married Miss Bell, and has five children—Robert, Charles, Grover, Bessie, and infant.

Eighth.—John Bledsoe married Miss Scoggins, and has four children—Cornelius, Creath, Anna Willie and Louisa.

Ninth.—Robert Winston died young.

Tenth.—George Smith died young.

Eleventh.—Virginia Louisa married Mr. Brashear, and has one son—Edwin.

OBSERVATIONS.

Mr. Edwin Winston Dabney emigrated from Kentucky to Kenneyville, Austin County, Texas, where he is now living with his wife and family (1887.)

RECORD NO. 98

(Supplied by Dr. Archie H. Dabney.)

Judge Thomas Catlett Dabney, son of Albert Gallatin Dabney and Miss Ann Eliza Catlett, and his wife, Miss Rumsey. Their children were:

SIXTH GENERATION.

First.—James Rumsey married Miss Curtis, and is living in Spokane Falls, Washington Territory. He has two sons, named Curtis and Thomas.

Second.—Lieut. Albert Jouett married Miss Tripp, of South Carolina; lives in Hopkinsville, Kentucky. Has two daughters— Martha and Bertha.

Third.—Cornelia married Mr. Averitt. She is dead, and left one son, J. B. Averitt.

Fourth.—Thomas C., Jr., died at twenty years, while in college.

Fifth.—Annie S., single, living in Cadiz, Kentucky, with her mother.

Sixth.—Minnie married Mr. Crenshaw; has four children, viz.: Susie, Rumsey, Dabney and Robert.

Seventh.—Edwin Frank married Miss Moore; has no children.

Eighth.—Archie Smith married Miss Vaughn in 1887. Miss Vaughn's mother was a Dade; her uncle was Dabney Dade.

Ninth.—Caroline Temple unmarried, living in Cadiz, Kentucky.

OBSERVATIONS.

The late Judge Thomas Catlett Dabney, of Cadiz, Kentucky, wrote: "My father, Albert Gallatin Dabney, deceased, moved from Louisa County, Virginia, in the fall of 1830, to Hopkinsville, Kentucky, where he lived and died, leaving a large family of sons and daughters, all of whom of those now living, save myself and a sister, Mrs. Juliette O. M. Price, of Auburn, Logan County, Kentucky, have moved to, and now reside in Austin, Goliad and Comanche Counties, Texas."

Charles William Dabney, of Dalton Junction, Hanover County, Virginia, says: " That long before Albert Dabney's emigration to Kentucky, there was settled in Jefferson County, Kentucky, a General ———- Dabney, whom he thinks must have been an uncle of Albert G. Dabney, and that he had children. Judge Thomas C. Dabney was born in Louisa County, Virginia, on the 20th of September, 1823, and died in 1886."

The following is his obituary; taken from a Cadiz, Kentucky paper: " Death is ever shocking, but no event ever occurred in Cadiz that shocked the entire community more than the announcement, last Friday morning, that Judge Dabney was dead. Just a week previous his erect and portly form was seen in the Court room, with the rosy tint of health upon his face; hence, when the announcement was made that he was dead, the news was shocking. He had only been sick six or seven days. On Friday, the 15th inst. he was taken sick, and against his own protestations, Dr. Crenshaw, the family physician, was called in, who, upon examination, found that he had pneumonia. His sons, Lieut. A. J. Dabney, of Hopkinsville, and Dr. A. S. Dabney, of Paducah, and his daughter, Miss Annie Dabney, who was on a visit to friends in Paducah, were summoned, and from the beginning of his sickness to his death he received every attention from his devoted friends." He was born in Louisa County, Virginia, on the 20th of September, 1823; hence was in the sixty-fourth year of his age (1886.)

At the early age of eighteen Judge Dabney commenced the study of law under the guidance of Judge Bradley. In the fall of 1854 he was granted license to practice his profession. He afterwards was elected County Attorney, which position he held for several years. He was also School Commissioner, and while acting in that capacity, re-districted the county. He was elected

County Judge in 1852, at the first election held under the new Constitution, and was elected Circuit Judge in 1857, and held that position until 1862, when he declined to stand for re-election. Since that time he has devoted his entire time to his profession, having been engaged in nearly every important case that has been tried in this county since his advent as an attorney, and frequently declined cases in other counties. Having been closely identified with Judge Dabney for the last eighteen years, and for six years of the time having been his law partner, we think that we are qualified to speak of his standing as an attorney. In our opinion no man in this end of the State ever won more reputation as an able, conscientious lawyer. He was always careful not to give a hasty opinion, always probing every question to the bottom; and where clients gave him an honest statement of the facts, he seldom gave an opinion that was not afterwards backed by the arbitrament of a court. He nearly always advised parties to settle their differences without appealing to the courts, invariably where the parties were related, and never advised suit unless he believed, beyond all doubt, that the party was in the right. When once he undertook a case he never flagged. He examined every paper, every pleading, and every exhibit connected with the case carefully, and the law pertaining to it, until he was perfectly familiar with it; and when once aroused to the justness of his client's cause, he often devoted months of unremitted labor where only a few hundred dollars were involved. His arguments in some cases exhibit great research, and were always listened to by the attorneys and court with marked attention.

Judge Dabney was a member of the Christian Church, and had been for the last forty years, and for the last decade had spent much of his time studying the Bible. He had been an elder of the church for over twenty years, and by the solicitation of the other elders, had always taken an active part in the devotional exercises, and in the absence of the minister, reading a chapter and making an explanatory talk upon it. He was, and had been for a number of years, an active Sunday School worker, teaching every Sunday the Bible class, and was identified with the South Kentucky Sunday School and Missionary Association, having been for a time President of that body, and for several years one of the executive members, making liberal contributions every year to aid it.

Mrs. Archie S. Dabney, *nee* Vaughn, has an uncle named Dabney Dade. (Mrs. Dabney's mother was a Dade).

RECORD NO. 99

(Supplied by Edwin Winston Dabney.)

Albert Smith Dabney, third son of Albert Gallatin Dabney, and Ann Eliza Catlett, and his wife, Pamelia Middleton.

SIXTH GENERATION.

First.—James Middleton married and lives in Louisville, Kentucky.

Second.—John Catlett married Miss Chappell; has children, and lives in Cadiz, Kentucky (1887).

Third.—Albert Smith married Miss Loos, of Bethany, Virginia.

Fourth.—Harriet married Mr. Roach, of Clarksville, Tennessee.

OBSERVATIONS.

Mr. Albert Smith Dabney died in Cadiz, Kentucky, in 1860.

RECORD NO. 100

(Supplied by Edwin Winston Dabney.)

Cornelius Isaac Dabney, fourth son of Albert Gallatin Dabney and Ann Eliza Catlett, and his wife, Susan Garnett.

SIXTH GENERATION.

First.—Albert Gallatin married Miss O. Harvey, and has seven children, viz.: Mary, Caroline, Margaret, Mattie, Sarah C., Albert, and an infant (1887).

Second.—James Smith married Miss Harvey, and has three children, viz.: Austin, Mary and Marcia.

Third.—Cornelius Isaac married Miss McNutt, and has five children, viz.: Smith, Brice, Robert, Bernice, and an infant.

Fourth.—Edwin M. married Miss Millar, and has one son named Couch and two daughters, Ella and Cleopa.

Fifth.—Dr. Henry Thomas, just married, 1887, to Miss Kiblinger, of Louisiana.

Sixth.—Fanny married Peter Hervey, and has seven children.

Seventh.—Susan unmarried.

Eighth.—Eustacia married Lou Hill, and has three children.

Ninth.—Annie unmarried.

RECORD NO. 101

(Supplied by Edward Winston Dabney.)

Walter Scates Dabney, oldest son of Albert Gallatin Dabney, and Elizabeth Scates, and his wife, Lucy Dickinson.

SIXTH GENERATION.

First.—William Spotswood.

Second.—Joseph.

Third.—Parker Ritchie.

Fourth.—Walter Edwin.

Mr. Walter Scates Dabney married a second time, Miss Texana Bibb, and had one daughter named Lucy.

OBSERVATIONS.

W. S. Dabney moved to Goliad, Texas, from Virginia, in 1872, and is now living there (1887).

RECORD NO. 102

(Supplied by Edward Winston Dabney.)

Joseph Whorton Dabney, second son of Albert Gallatin Dabney and Elizabeth Scates, and his wife, Lucy Ann Bowles.

SIXTH GENERATION.

First.—Joseph.

Second.—Augustus.

Third.—Elizabeth.

Fourth.—Walter.

Fifth.—Lucy.

Joseph Whorton Dabney is living at date (1887).

RECORD NO. 103

(Supplied by William Winston Dabney.)

Richard Dabney, fourth son of William and Philadelphia Dabney, and Diana Guathmey, his wife. Their children were:

FOURTH GENERATION.

First.—Richard married Miss Fanny Dabney, daughter of Isaac Dabney, his uncle.

Second.—Temple married Miss Guathmey.

Third.—Joseph unmarried.

Fourth.—Isaac unmarried.

Fifth.—Benjamin unmarried.

Sixth.—Henry married Miss Jackson.

Seventh.—Owen unmarried.

Eighth.—Lucy married Mr. Merritt.

Ninth.—Hannah Temple married William Dabney, son of Isaac.

Tenth.—Anna unmarried.

RECORD NO. 104

(Supplied by William Winston Dabney.)

William Dabney, fifth son of William and Philadelphia Dabney, and his wife, Sallie Guathmey. Their children were:

FOURTH GENERATION.

First.—Cornelius married Diana Dabney, daughter of William, son of Isaac Dabney and Hannah Temple Dabney, his cousin.

Second.—William D.

Third.—Bushrod Washington.

Fourth.—Mordecai Booth.

Fifth.—Martha Washington.

RECORD NO. 105

(Supplied by William Winston Dabney.)

Guathmey Dabney, sixth son of William and Philadelphia Dabney, and his wife, Miss Mordecai. Their children were:

FOURTH GENERATION.

First.—James.

Second.—John.

Third.—Mordecai.

Fourth.—Sarah.

Fifth.—Nancy.

Sixth.—Elizabeth.

RECORD NO. 106

(Given by William Winston Dabney, obtained by him by letter from John Mercer Waller long since.)

John Dabney, son of Cornelius and Sarah Jennens Dabney, and his wife, Anna Harris.   Their children were:

THIRD GENERATION.

First—Sarah, born 1746; married Thomas Waller, and was grandmother of Colonel John Mercer Waller, who supplied this record.   Mrs. Waller died in 1822.

Second.—Mary married Thomas Minor.

Third.—William married Miss Quarles, and they were the parents of John Quarles Dabney.

Fourth.—John married Miss Anna Harris and Miss Margaret Smith, of North Carolina, and was known as John Dabney, of Albemarle.

Fifth.—Anna married Henry Terrell.

Sixth.—Elizabeth married Bernard Brown, and was the mother of Dr. Charles Brown.

Seventh.—Susan married Thomas Harris.

Eighth.—Lucy married Thomas McReynolds, and was the mother of James and Dabney McReynolds.

Ninth.—Rebecca married Thomas Warren, and was the mother of Colonel Robert Warren.

Tenth.—Cornelius married Miss Harris; moved to Shelbyville, Kentucky.

Eleventh.—Nancy married John Hunter.

CHART OF JOHN DABNEY, OF SPOTTSYLVANIA (SECOND SON OF CORNELIUS D'AUBIGNE AND SARAH JENNINGS).

2d Generation.	3d Generation.
1. John Dabney.	
	2. Sarah Dabney.
	3. Mary Dabney.
	4. William Dabney.
	5. John Dabney.
	6. Anna Dabney.
	7. Elizabeth Dabney.
	8. Susan Dabney.
	9. Lucy Dabney.
	10. Rebecca Dabney.
	11. Cornelius Dabney.
	12. Nancy Dabney.
	13. Daughter, married Flournoy.

Anna Harris

No. on Chart.	Index.	No. Gen.	No. Record.
1	John Dabney and Anna Harris............	2	106
2	Sarah Dabney and Thomas Waller........	4	107
3	William Dabney and Miss Quarles.........	4	109
	John Quarles Dabney and his two wives....	5	110
5	John Dabney, of Albemarle, and Margaret Smith...................................	4	111
	Dabney Waller and Elizabeth Minor......	5	108

OBSERVATIONS.

Doctor William Wall Dabney, of Lodi, Mississippi, and who is a grandson of John Dabney, of Albemarle, above, states that there was another daughter who married Flournoy, the original settler of that name.

The foregoing record is doubtless that of John Dabney, and was given in a letter to William Winston Dabney by the late Colonel John Mercer Waller, and may be considered a correct one from the many confirmations of it given by Dr. William Wall Dabney, who says, speaking of his grandfather, John Dabney, of Albemarle: "My great grandfather's name was John, I think, but am not sure, and the original emigrant was his father or grandfather. I know but little of grandfather Dabney, and do not know that he had any brothers. I remember to have heard that he had a sister, who married a Mr. McReynolds. I knew James McReynolds, of Daingerfield, Texas, and also remember to have seen his brother, Dabney McReynolds, when I was a child. Flournoy, who was the progenitor of that name, married a Dabney, a sister to my grandfather; and the father of Colonel Thomas Warren married another sister. The venerable Dr. Charles Brown, of Albemarle County, Virginia, who attended the convention of the Jenning Dabneys, at Mr. John Mercer Waller's house, after the war, was a first cousin of my father (Charles Anderson Dabney, son of John Dabney, of Albemarle").

Dr. William Wall Dabney does not mention that John Dabney, his grandfather, married Anna Harris. This may possibly have been an error of Colonel J. M. Waller, or he may have married Miss Harris, and she died soon after marriage, and without children, and he removed to North Carolina, and there married Margaret Smith, as stated by Dr. Dabney.

Confirmation as to the correctness of Mr. J. M. Waller's record comes from another quarter. Francis M. Dabney, of Barry, Illinois, states: "My father was John Quarles Dabney, who was the son of William Dabney, who married Miss Quarles; hence his middle name, and I am descended from John Dabney, the original emigrant."   (In this he is mistaken; he, John Dabney, being the son of the original emigrant, Cornelius d'Aubigné).

The family register of the Wallers, now in the possession of the widow of Colonel John Mercer Waller (herself also a Dabney, being the daughter of William and Jemima Dabney), states that Mrs. Sarah Waller, *nee* Dabney, was born in 1746, which date indicates that she was of the third generation, and therefore that she must have been a daughter of John Dabney, as we have the records of his two brothers, William and Cornelius, the first supplied by Mr. William Winston Dabney, and the second by Judge William Pope Dabney.

Mr. Charles William Dabney has stated positively that Cornelius d'Aubigné married Sarah Jennings in 1721. Cornelius d'Aubigné's will gives his son, John, as his second son, and as such, he could not have been born before 1723-4, perhaps later, therefore he must have married when very young. He was one of the executors of his father's will, together with Henry Terrell, who, perhaps, may have been the father of Henry Terrell, who married John Dabney's daughter, Anna Dabney.

Mr. Dorsay, of Washington, states: "That one Cornelius Dabney was a soldier in the Revolutionary War, and fought under the command of Captain Terrell. It seems probable that he was Cornelius, the son of John Dabney, and Terrell, his brother-in-law."

RECORD NO. 107

(Given by Mrs. John Mercer Waller.)

Sarah Dabney, daughter of John Dabney and Anna Harris, and Thomas Waller.

FOURTH GENERATION.

First.—Anna married Joel Harris.

Second.—Agnes married Sharp Smith.

Third.—Sarah married Joseph Spicer.

Fourth.—Carr died in 1843, unmarried.

Fifth.—Dabney born February 20th, 1772. Died June 6th, 1849. Married Elizabeth Minor, daughter of Thomas and Mary Minor.

Sixth.—Pomfret.

Seventh.—Dorothy.

Eighth.—John.

Ninth.—Elizabeth.

Tenth.—Mary.

OBSERVATIONS.

Mr. Waller was a descendant of John Waller, of England, who emigrated to Virginia in Colonial times. He was a son of John and Agnes Waller, and was born July, 1732, and died in 1788, aged fifty-six years. His widow, Mrs. Sarah (Dabney) Waller survived him many years, and died in 1822.

Mr. John Mercer Waller, grandson of the above, was born in 1814. He married first, Dorothea Rowzie; second, Martha Pomfret Waller; third, Annie Elizabeth Waller, *nee* Dabney, a daughter of William and Jemima Dabney, and widow of William Carr Waller. Mr. Waller was a great believer in the Jennings' estate, and was, with Dr. Brown, one of the most active promoters of the re-unions of the claimants, one of which was held at his house after the war. Mr. Waller is now dead, and his widow is living at Chilesburg, Virginia (1887).

RECORD NO. 108

Given by Mrs. John Mercer Waller.)

Dabney Waller, son of Thomas Waller and Sarah Dabney, and Elizabeth Minor.

FIFTH GENERATION.

First.—Thomas Carr married Miss Waller; moved to Kentucky, and had a large family.

Second.—Sarah Minor died unmarried, in her seventy-second year.

Third.—Dabney Washington married Caroline Pleasants, and settled in Caroline County, Virginia.

Fourth.—Mary Ann died unmarried, in her fifty-sixth year.

Fifth.—Elizabeth.

Sixth.—Agnes Carr married Pike Pollard, and died in her thirty-third year.

RECORD NO. 109

William Dabney, son of John Dabney, of Spottsylvania, Virginia, and grandson of Cornelius and Sarah Jennings Dabney, and his wife, Miss Quarles. Only one son is known to me, viz.:

FOURTH GENERATION.

First.—John Quarles, born in 1760, was first married in 1794, and second time in 1817, near Richmond, Kentucky. Died 1832.

OBSERVATIONS.

Francis M. Dabney, of Barry, Illinois, who gives the above record, says: "My grandfather's name was William, and he married a Miss Quarles, from whom my father, John Quarles Dabney, took his middle name. He resided in Spottsylvania, Virginia. Cornelius Dabney, of Shelbyville, Kentucky, was his brother, and my father's uncle. There was Colonel Roger Quarles and Judge Ambrose Quarles.

RECORD NO. 110

John Quarles Dabney, son of William Dabney and Miss Quarles, and his first wife. Name not known.

There were three children, names unknown; the oldest was born in 1795.

His first wife having died, late in life, after his children were grown up, and when he was fifty-seven years of age, he married a young lady of seventeen, younger than his children, and they had nine children, the youngest being Francis M. Dabney, of Barry, Illinois, who has furnished this record, but does not name any of his brothers and sisters, or his half-brothers and sisters. He states: "My father, John Q. Dabney, was a private in the Revolutionary War, and served under General Greene."

Mr. J. Q. Dabney was a missionary Baptist preacher, and died of cholera in 1832.

Francis M. Dabney, his youngest son and youngest child, by his second wife, was born in 1831. He says: "I remember in 1862, while in the Union army, I captured a man near West Plain, Missouri, whose name was Dabney. He claimed to be of the family of Robert Dabney, and knew all the history of the older ancestors, about as I have always understood it myself, by which I knew that he must be of the same family."

The following was taken from a Chicago paper (1888).

MRS. SARAH B. DABNEY.

ONE OF THE TWO KNOWN REVOLUTIONARY WIDOWS LIVING IN ILLINOIS.

PITTSFIELD, ILL., Jan. 13.—[Special.]—Mrs. Sarah B. Dabney of Barry, this county, one of the two well known widows of Revolutionary soldiers living in this State, was born near Richmond, Kentucky, December 25, 1799. In her eighteenth year she was united in marriage with John Q. Dabney, near where she was born. They remained in Kentucky until 1833, when her husband died. To them were born nine children, two of whom are living, one at Barry, Illinois, and the other at Kinderhook, this State. Mrs. Dabney remained a widow, and in 1853 came to Barry, this county, to live with her son, Francis, and with whom she still makes it her home. She has been drawing a pension of $12 per month since 1853. Mrs. Dabney is a woman of small stature,

weighing perhaps ninety-five pounds, but has been possessed of a
wonderful constitution, for, notwithstanding a life of peculiar trials
and privations in an early day, and her extreme old age, she yet
persists in performing her own household duties even to her wash-
ing. She has enjoyed remarkably good health all her life, and
to-day, barring her nearly total deafness, is a fine specimen of good,
ripe old age.

John Q. Dabney, the late husband of the subject of this sketch,
was born in Gloucester County, Virginia, about the year 1760,
where he resided until he went into the Revolutionary War. His
widow and son have no record of the time of his enlistment, or of
the time he was in the service. They only know he was a private,
and think he was in the command of General Greene, of the
Department of the South. Mr. Dabney's marriage with his surviving widow was his second, and by a little figuring it will be
seen that it was a union of youth and old age, she being eighteen,
and he fifty-seven. It will also be noticed that he lived to the good
old age of seve y-three before departing this life.

<h3 style="text-align:center">RECORD NO. III</h3>

(Given by Dr. William Wall Dabney, of Lodi, Mississippi.)

John Dabney, of Albemarle County, Virginia, son of John
Dabney 2d, and Anna Harris, and his wife, Miss Margaret Smith,
of North Carolina.

<h4 style="text-align:center">FIFTH GENERATION.</h4>

First.—John married Sarah Cox.

Second.—Anna married Dr. George W. Bennett, of North
Carolina.

Third.—Elizabeth (Betsey) married Edward Warren.

Fourth.—William married Eliza Hicks, of Williamson County,
Tennessee. No children.

Fifth.—Nancy married William Bond, of Williamson County,
Tennessee.

Sixth.—Margarette O. married Robert McLemore, of Williamson County, Tennessee.

Seventh.—Mary (Polly) married John House, of Williamson County, Tennessee.

Eighth.—Charles Anderson married Nancy Portress Wall, daughter of William Wall, of Rockingham County, North Carolina.

Ninth.—Bethinia married Atkins Jefferson McLemore, of Williamson County, Tennessee.

OBSERVATIONS.

Dr. William Wall Dabney, of Lodi, Montgomery County, Mississippi, writes: " My great grandfather, John Dabney, was born in Albemarle County, Virginia. He served in the Revolutionary War, and was at the surrender of Cornwallis, at Yorktown. He emigrated to North Carolina, Chatham County, and settled on Deep River, where he married Miss Elizabeth Smith, the daughter of Lemuel Smith, Sr., of North Carolina. He represented his county in the Legislature for fourteen years, and subsequently removed with his family and other relatives to Middle Tennessee, and bought land, and settled three miles from Franklin, Williamson County, Tennessee, where he lived and died, at an advanced age, between eighty-five and eighty-six years, respected and beloved by all who knew him. My great grandfather's name, I think, was John, but do not know. The original emigrant—— ——was his father or grandfather. I knew but little of grandfather Dabney, and do not know that he had any brothers. I remember to have heard that he had a sister who married James McReynolds, of Daingerfield, Texas, and I also recollect seeing his brother Dabney McReynolds, when I was a child. Flournoy, of Kentucky, who was the progenitor of that name, married a Dabney, a sister to my grandfather; and the father of Colonel Robert Warren married another sister."

RECORD

(Supplied by Robert S. Dabney, of Hernando, Mississippi.)

Mr. Robert S. Dabney, of Hernando, Mississippi, writes: "I will refer you to my father for all the information you desire. His name is John O. Dabney, Cornersville, Giles County, Tennessee. He has two brothers, R. C. Dabney, Lewisburg, Marshall County, Tennessee, and Charles A. Dabney, same post-office as my father's. I have learned that all the Dabneys in the United States of America are related, and also that they are descended from Cornelius Dabney. Our branch of the Dabney family felt an interest in the Jennings' estate in England, when I was a boy, but nothing ever came of it. Then it was the family was traced back to its origin— the United States. One Charles Brown used to correspond with my grandfather, John Dabney, and gave him all the information he had about that estate. Charles Brown lived in Virginia, and was a Dabney on his mother's side."

CHART OF JOHN DABNEY, OF ALBEMARLE COUNTY, VIRGINIA.*

Probably 3d Generation.	*4th Generation.*
John Dabney, of Albemarle.	1. John Dabney.
	2. Anna Dabney.
	3. Betsey Dabney.
	4. William Dabney.
	5. Nancy Dabney.
	6. Margarette Dabney.
	7. Mary Dabney.
	8. Charles Anderson Dabney.
	9. Bethinia Dabney.
Margaret Smith.	

No. on Chart.	Index.	No. Gen.	No. Record.
1	John Dabney (see his record) and Susan Cox	4	112
2	Anna Dabney and Dr. George W. Bennett.	4	113
3	Betsey Dabney and Edward Warren.......	4	114
4	William Dabney...........................		
6	Margarette O. Dabney and Robert McLemore.................................	4	116
7	Mary Dabney and John House............	4	117
8	Charles Anderson Dabney and Nancy Portress Wall...........................	4	118
9	Bethinia Dabney and Atkins Jefferson McLemore.............................	4	120

*Supposed grandson of John Dabney, the second son of Cornelius and Sarah Jennings Dabney.

John Dabney emigrated to Deep River, North Carolina, and after many years' residence there, removed to Franklin, Williamson County, Tennessee, with his family, and there died. He is supposed to have been the son of John Dabney, who was the second son of Cornelius and Sarah Jennings Dabney, the original settlers in Virginia.

RECORD NO. 113

(Supplied by Dr. William Wall Dabney, of Lodi, Mississippi.)

John Dabney, the oldest son of John Dabney and Margaret Smith, and his wife, Sarah Cox.

FIFTH GENERATION.

First.—William Pressly unmarried; living (1877) in Hernando, Mississippi; over eighty years of age.

Second.—John Overton married Miss Day, of Giles County, Tennessee; is living (1887), at eighty years of age, in Cornersville, Tennessee, and is the father of Robert S. Dabney, of Hernando, Mississippi.

Third.—Sarah married Dr. Haywood, son of Judge Haywood, of Nashville, Tennessee; had children.

Fourth.—Robert Cox married Miss Narcissa Hunter, of Williamson County, Tennessee, and is living at date (1887); had children.

Fifth.—Martha married Pryor Smith, and died young, and left no children.

Sixth.—Margaret married Colonel G. W. Day, now of Humboldt, West Tennessee, and has children.

Seventh.—Charles Anderson married a Miss Cox. They reside at Cornersville, Tennessee, and have no children.

OBSERVATIONS.

Judge Haywood above mentioned was, perhaps, the first Judge of the Circuit Court of Middle Tennessee, after it began to be settled.

RECORD NO. 113

(Supplied by Dr. William Wall Dabney.)

Dr. George W. Bennett and Anna Dabney, oldest daughter of John Dabney and Margaret Smith.

FIFTH GENERATION.

First.—John Dabney married Elizabeth Terrell, of Williamson County, Tennessee. They have many children living in that county,

Second.—Jane married Henry Hunter, of Williamson County, Tennessee. There were five children, viz.: John, George, Julia, Agnes and Sophronia.

Third.—Joseph W. married Narcissa Ricord, of Giles County, Tennessee. They raised no children.

Fourth.—Elizabeth married James Kennedy, of Maury County, Tennessee; no children.

Fifth.—George William died unmarried, of cancer.

Sixth.—Margaret married Thomas Brown, of Williamson County, Tennessee, and had children.

Seventh—Dolly married Isaac Briggs, of Williamson County, Tennessee, and had many children.

Eighth.—Bethinia married Thompson Cunningham, of Maury County, Tennessee, and had children.

OBSERVATIONS.

Dr. W. W. Dabney, of Lodi, Mississippi, states: "Nearly all of my aunt Anna Bennett's children live in Williamson County, Tennessee, where I was born, and where my grandfather, John Dabney, settled, when he emigrated from Chatham County, North Carolina, to Tennessee. Dr. Bennett came with him to Tennessee perhaps ninety or hundred years ago.

RECORD NO. 114

(Supplied by Dr. William Wall Dabney.)

Edward Warren and Elizabeth Dabney, third child of John Dabney and Margaret Smith.

FIFTH GENERATION.

First.—John Dabney married Mary Crouch, of Williamson County, Tennessee, and had a large family.

Second.—Allen married Mary North, of Williamson County, Tennessee, and had a large family.

Third.—Patsy married Jonathan Smith, of Marshall County, Tennessee, and had a large family, and subsequently emigrated to Hinds County, Mississippi.

Fourth.—Sarah married Thomas Bond, and had a family.

Fifth.—Margaret married John House, of Williamson County, Tennessee, and had two children, Honorable John Ford House, ex-Member of Congress from Clarksville District, Tennessee, and Martha, who married Isham Lacele, of Williamson County, Tennessee.

Sixth.—Nancy married John Herron, of Williamson County, Tennessee; had a large family, and emigrated to Tallahatchie County, Mississippi.

Seventh.—Lydia married Rev. Andrew Herron, of Williamson County, Tennessee; subsequently emigrated to Marshall County, Mississippi, and thence to Guadalupe, Texas, and have a large family living in latter place.

Eighth.—William married Miss Malone, of Marshall County, Mississippi, and has children living at, and in that place.

Ninth.—Susan married a Mr. Elliot, of Mississippi, and lives in De Soto County, Mississippi, and has children.

Tenth.—Mary married Hon. Edward Warren, of Camden, Arkansas, ex-Member of Congress, and has a family.

OBSERVATIONS.

Mr. Warren was a native of North Carolina; was married there, and came to Tennessee when his father-in-law came.

RECORD NO. 115
(Supplied by Dr. William Wall Dabney.)

William Bond and Nancy Dabney, fifth child of John Dabney and Margaret Smith.

FIFTH GENERATION.

First.—Sidney died unmarried at Paris, Tennessee, where he was an accomplished and successful merchant.

Second.—Margaret married Richard Maury, brother of Lieut. M. F. Maury, formerly of the United States Navy and Washington Observatory. They had children.

Third.—Lucy married Thomas Hughes, of Williamson County, Tennessee, and had a family.

Fourth.—Elizabeth married Segar McLemore, of Madison County, Tennessee, and died young, leaving two or three children.

Fifth.—Thomas H. married Mary Banks, of Williamson County, Tennessee; had a family, and accumulated a fortune.

Sixth.—William married Miss Mayberry, of Williamson County, Tennessee, and had children.

Seventh.—John Dabney married a lady of Jackson, West Tennessee.

Eighth.—Bethinia married John Farris, of Kentucky.

Ninth.—Ann married (name of husband not known).

Robert and Frank Bond live in Jackson, Tennessee, and are married.

RECORD NO. 116

(Supplied by Dr. William Wall Dabney.)

Robert McLemore and Margarette O. Dabney, sixth child of John Dabney and Margaret Smith.

FIFTH GENERATION.

First.—John Dabney married Elizabeth Marr, of Tuscaloosa, Alabama, and had four children.

Second.—Mary Minor married William O. Perkins, of Williamson County, Tennessee, and had children.

Third.—Robert Weakly married Harriet Figures, of Franklin County, Tennessee, and had a large family.

Fourth.—Margaret Smith married General Fontaine Maury de Graffenreid, of Williamson County, Tennessee, and had a large family.

L

RECORD NO. 117

(Supplied by Dr. William Wall Dabney.)

John House and Mary Dabney, seventh child of John Dabney and Margaret Smith.

FIFTH GENERATION.

First.—Robert M.

Second.—Lemuel S.

Third.—Elizabeth.

Mrs. House died young, and Mr. House married for a second wife, his wife's niece, Margaret Warren.

RECORD NO. 118

(Supplied by Dr. William Wall Dabney.)

Charles Anderson Dabney, eighth child of John Dabney and Margaret Smith, and Nancy Portress Wall.

FIFTH GENERATION.

First.—William Wall married first, Mary A. Ingram, of Hardeman County, Tennessee; second, Miss Luty Morton, of Williamson County, daughter of Jacob Morton, Sr.; third, Miss Collins, daughter of Judge W. Y. Collins, of Carroll County, Mississippi.

Second.—Lucy Ann married Henry F. Atkins, of Henry County, Western Tennessee, and had a large family.

Third.—Margarette Smith married Dr. Hezekiah Terrell, of Williamson County, Tennessee, and had several children.

Fourth.—John Overton married Tabitha C. Morton, daughter of Jacob Morton, Sr., of Tennessee, formerly of Virginia. They had two children—Maritta and Samuel Morton Dabney, of Bolivar, Mississippi.

Fifth.—Mary Elizabeth died at fourteen years of age, of consumption.

Sixth.—Ann Portress married Samuel S. Morton, and died young, leaving five children.

OBSERVATIONS.

Miss Nancy Portress Wall above was the daughter of William Wall, of Rockingham County, North Carolina. After Mr. Wall's death, his wife married Thomas Cash, of North Carolina, and emigrated to Williamson County, Tennessee, where C. A. Dabney was married to Miss Wall in 1814 or 1815, and where they both lived and died.

OBSERVATIONS.

(Supplied by Samuel Morton Dabney, of Bolivar, Mississippi.)

Samuel Morton Dabney, son of above John O. Dabney, writes from Bolivar County, Mississippi (Wareland Plantation): "I was born at Franklin, Williamson County, Tennessee. My father was John O. Dabney, a son of Charles A. Dabney. My grandfather, Charles A. Dabney, came from Virginia, and settled three miles west of Franklin. My mother was a daughter of Jacob Morton. He also came from Virginia. You can get the entire Records of both families from Dr. W. W. Dabney. He is the oldest son of the family living. He lives in Lodi, Mississippi, or you can write to Mrs. Margaret Terrell, at Carter's Creek Station, Maury County, Tennessee. She is a sister of my father."

Mr. J. Watson Woods, of Memphis, who is a Dabney on his mother's side, writes: "These two John O. Dabneys were cousins."

RECORD NO. 119

(Supplied by Dr. William Wall Dabney.)

William Wall Dabney, M. D., of Lodi, Mississippi, Montgomery County, oldest son of Charles Anderson Dabney and Nancy Portress Wall, and his wife, Mary Ann Ingram.

SIXTH GENERATION.

First.—Needham Ingram, who was wounded at Gettysburg, which eventually caused his death.

Dr. W. W. Dabney married a second wife, Miss Luty Morton, daughter of James Morton, Sr. She died eighteen months after marriage. No children. He then married a third time, Miss Collins, daughter of Judge W. Y. Collins, of Carroll County, Mississippi. Their children were:

First.—Linda M.

Second.—Elisha Bartlett.

Third.—Camelina.

Fourth.—William Wall.

Fifth.—Bessie.

All unmarried, and living with their parents in Lodi, Mississippi at present date (1887).

RECORD NO. 120

(Supplied by Dr. William Wall Dabney.)

Atkins Jefferson McLemore and Bethinia Dabney, ninth child of John Dabney and Margaret Smith.

FIFTH GENERATION.

First.—Robert Anderson married first, Ann McCurren, who died, leaving several children; second, he married Miss Kinnard, of Williamson county.

Second.—Margaret Williams married John T. Word, of same county, and had four children. She is living at date (1887), a widow.

Third.—Ann married Thomas B. Bond, of Williamson County, Tennessee. They had a large family.

Fourth.—John Dabney married a Miss Pope, and has several children.

Fifth.—William S., a lawyer and Judge of the Circuit Court of his district, Franklin, Tennessee. Married a daughter of Dr. Wain, of Nashville. They have children.

Sixth.—Dr. Sidney married Miss Hobbs, of Franklin, Tennessee. He died young, leaving a wife and two or three children.

Seventh—Bethinia Jefferson married William Bond, and emigrated to Texas. They have a family.

Eighth.—Elizabeth Minor married James C. Alexander, of Maury County, and had a family.

Ninth.—Lemuel married a Miss Frierson, of Columbia, Maury County, Tennessee, and has children.

RECORD NO. 121

(Supplied by Judge William Pope Dabney.

Cornelius Dabney 2d, son of Cornelius d'Aubigné, or Dabney, and Sarah Jennings, or Jennens, and his wife, Mary Lucy Winston.

THIRD GENERATION.

First.—John, known as John Dabney, of Appomattox, married Miss Harris, daughter of Colonel Harris, of Louisa County, Virginia.

Second.—William.

These are the only ones I know of. John's record will be seen further on; but I have no records of William, and think he could not have married, or if he did, that he left no children.

OBSERVATIONS.

Judge William Pope Dabney, of Powhatan, Virginia, states: " That Cornelius Dabney, the son of Cornelius and Sarah Jennings, or Jennens Dabney, was Inspector of Tobacco, at Page's Warehouse, on the Pamunky River, which, as tobacco notes were currency in Virginia in those days, and a legal tender, was a position of high trust and great importance; and that he lived and died at this place before his father died, leaving a widow and small children" These are mentioned in Cornelius Dabney, Sr.'s will.

CHART OF CORNELIUS DABNEY 2D (THIRD SON OF CORNELIUS D'AUBIGNE AND SARAH JENNINGS) AND HIS SON JOHN.

2d Generation.	3d Generation.	4th Generation.
Cornelius Dabney 2d.	John Dabney, of Appomattox.	
		1. Garland Dabney.
		2. Mrs. Wisdom.
		3. Mrs. Le Grand.
		4. Anderson Dabney.
		5. Daughter, eloped.
		6. Mrs. Harris.
		7. Mrs. Lutheum.
		8. Tyree Dabney.
		9. Nathaniel Dabney.
		10. Robert Kelso Dabney.
		11. John Dabney.
		12. Cornelius Dabney.
	Ann Harris.	
William Dabney.		
Lucy Winston.		

No. on Chart.	Index.	No. Gen.	No. Record.
	John Dabney, of Appomattox, and Ann Harris	4	122
1	Garland Dabney	5	123
4	Anderson Dabney and Hannah Bennett	5	124
	William Harris Dabney and Martha B. Williams	6	125
8	Tyree Dabney	5	126
10	Robert Kelso Dabney and Lucy Ann Pope	5	127
	Judge William Pope Dabney and Miss Lula Madison	6	128
	Robert Dabney and Ann Marye	6	129

RECORD NO. 122

(Supplied by Judge William Pope Dabney and William Harris Dabney.)

John Dabney, of Appomattox, son of Cornelius Dabney 2d, and Lucy Winston, and his wife, Ann Harris; born 1740; died 1830, aged ninety years.

FOURTH GENERATION.

First.—Garland married, and moved to Georgia, and became there a wealthy planter.

Second.—A daughter married Mr. Wisdom, and went to North Carolina; had children.

Third.—A daughter married John Le Grand. They lived in Prince Edward County, Virginia, and their children went South and West.

Fourth.—Anderson married Hannah Bennett, and moved to Georgia.

Fifth.—A daughter, who eloped with her father's overseer. They went South, and prospered greatly.

Sixth.—A daughter married a Mr. Harris, overseer of a large plantation on the Upper James River. They left a family.

Seventh.—A daughter married Robert Linthicun, of Buckingham County, Virginia, who was a near relative of Hon. Thomas S. Bocock, M. C. They left a family.

Eighth.—Tyree married and went to Alexandria, Louisiana (Red River), and was a merchant in that place.

Ninth.—Nathaniel was also a merchant of Alexandria, Louisiana, and died in that place of yellow fever; unmarried.

Tenth.—Robert Kelso, born 1787; died 1867, aged eighty years; married first, Miss Woodson, a daughter of Colonel Charles Woodson, a large planter in Cumberland County; second, Miss Lucy Ann Pope, only child of Colonel William Pope, of Montpelier, Powhatan County, Virginia.

Eleventh.—John moved to and settled in Kentucky.

Twelfth.—Cornelius died in the war of 1812, with England.

OBSERVATIONS.

Judge William Pope Dabney, who gave the above record, down to his father, Robert Kelso Dabney, states that there were twelve children, but could not remember the other two, neither could he remember the names of any of the daughters, but only the names of their husbands. The two last named sons were supplied by Mr. William Harris Dabney, of Rome, Georgia.

Mr. C. W. Dabney, of Dalton Junction, Virginia, states that long before Albert Gallatin Dabney moved to Kentucky, a General Dabney had gone there and settled, and had left descendants there. May he not have been the above John Dabney?

Judge William Pope Dabney, of Powhatan, Virginia, states: " My paternal grandfather, John Dabney, the son of Cornelius Dabney, was born in Hanover, near, or at Page's Warehouse, now known as Hanover Town, near Dabney's Ferry, across the Pamunky River, which separates the counties of Hanover and King William. At an early age he married Miss Harris, a daughter of Colonel Harris, of Louisa County, Virginia, and settled in Prince Edward County, at the Hermitage, near Walker's Church. About the year 1846, portions of Buckingham, Charlotte, and Prince Edward Counties were made into the new County of Appomattox, and the Hermitage is in the neighborhood of the place of General Lee's surrender. My grandfather purchased and owned a large tract of poor land, and raised a very large family. Like

most of the old Virginia landowners and slaveholders, it was somewhat of a struggle to support his large family, and he was unable
to give them more than a limited and practical education, and they
each left the paternal mansion so early that at no time in the lifetime of my grandmother, who lived to the advanced age of nearly
100 years, and who died at the old place, having survived her husband many years, were all the children together at the same time
in the old home. My grandfather was always known as 'the
best man in Prince Edward County.'"

Mrs. Dabney died about 1838. Mrs. Dabney was ninety years
of age at death, and must have been born about 1740. Mr.
Dabney had preceded her from fifteen to twenty years, and died
an old man—say seventy, which would make him to have been
born about the same time as his wife.

RECORD NO. 123

(Supplied by William Harris Dabney.)

Garland Dabney, oldest son of John Dabney, of Appomattox,
and Ann Harris, and his wife.

FIFTH GENERATION.

First.—John married, went to Mississippi, and died long ago.

Second.—Anderson married, went to Alabama, and died long
ago.

Third.—William married, and died in DeKalb County,
Georgia; no issue.

Fourth.—Ann married Mr. Hayes, and moved to Alabama or
Mississippi.

Fifth.—Narcissa married, and moved away.

Sixth.—Harriet married, and went to Mississippi.

OBSERVATIONS.

Garland Dabney moved to Georgia at the same time that his
brothers Anderson and Tyree did, and became a wealthy planter.

RECORD NO. 124

(Supplied by William Harris Dabney.)

Anderson Dabney, son of John Dabney, of Appomattox, and Ann Harris, and his wife, Hannah Bennett.

FIFTH GENERATION.

First.—Ann Harris married Thomas M. Dunrael, and is dead (1887).

Second.—Emma Eliza married. James M. Cullum, a lawyer, and both died in Atlanta, before the war.

Third.—Anderson Winston was a lawyer; settled in Macon, Georgia, and died before the war.

Fourth.—Tyree James was also a lawyer; settled in Alexandria, Louisiana, and died in Cuba before the war.

Fifth.—William Harris married Miss Martha B. Williams, daughter of Ami and Laura Williams, in Decatur, 1842. Mrs. Dabney died in Rome, Georgia, in 1885.

Sixth.—Elizabeth Antoniette married James W. Kirkpatrick, and resides in Decatur, DeKalb County, Georgia, in 1887.

OBSERVATIONS.

Mr. William Harris Dabney, of Rome, Georgia, writes: " My father, Anderson Dabney, came from Prince Edward County, Virginia, I think, when he was quite a young man, and settled in Green County, Georgia, and there married Miss Hannah Bennett, of Wilkes County, and bought and settled on a plantation in Jasper County, Georgia. I remember having heard that my father had several brothers, to-wit: Robert, John, Garland, Tyree, Cornelius and Nathaniel; but I never saw but three of them, namely, Garland, Tyree, and Nathaniel. Garland and Tyree came to Georgia when young men, and made their homes there, but both of them died several years before the Civil War. Nathaniel settled in Alexandria, Louisiana, and died there many years ago. Cornelius died in the last war with England. I do not know what became of Robert and John. I know nothing of father's sisters, but remember to have heard it said that one of them married a gentleman by the name of Harris, in Virginia."

RECORD NO. 125

(Supplied by William Harris Dabney.)

William Harris Dabney, son of Anderson Dabney and Hannah Bennett, and his wife, Miss Martha B. Williams. They have five children now living, viz.:

SIXTH GENERATION.

First.—William Anderson, a Presbyterian minister, residing near Lexington, Virginia, 1887.

Second.—Tyree James, residing in Baltimore.

Third.—Frank B., a civil engineer, residing in San Miguel, Mexico, at present time (1887).

Fourth.—John W., also a civil engineer, now on the Atlanta and Florida Railroad, in construction, 1887.

OBSERVATIONS.

Mr. William H. Dabney is a practicing attorney-at-law, in Rome, Georgia, 1887, under the firm of Dabney & Fouche.

RECORD NO. 126

(Supplied by William Harris Dabney.)

Tyree Dabney, son of John Dabney, of Appomattox, and Ann Harris, and his wife.

FIFTH GENERATION.

First.—James married, but left no family.

Second.—Tyree married, and left a family. He lived in Newton County, Georgia.

Third.—John married, and left a family. He also lived in Newton County, Georgia.

Fourth.—Ann Jane married Mr. Starrs, and lived in Austin County, six miles from Carrington, the county seat.

OBSERVATIONS.

Tyree Dabney moved to Alexandria, on the Red River, Louisiana, and was a merchant there.

RECORD NO. 127
(Given by Judge William Pope Dabney.)

Robert Kelso Dabney, son of John Dabney, of Appomattox, and Miss Harris, and his wife, Lucy Ann Pope.

FIFTH GENERATION.

First.—Judge William Pope; born about 1829. Married Miss Lula Madison, a niece of President James Madison; living at present time (1887), at Powhatan Court House.

Second.—Robert married Miss Marye, and died in Tennessee in 1876, at Sewanee University of the South. His children are much scattered.

These were the only children.

OBSERVATIONS.

Mr. Robert K. Dabney was twice married; his first wife was a daughter of Colonel Charles Woodson, a large planter of Cumberland; she died without issue. He then married Miss Pope, daughter and only child of Colonel William Pope, of Montpelier, Powhatan, the intimate bosom friend of William Wirt. (See Kennedy's Life of Wirt for notices of their correspondence.) Mr. R. K. Dabney commenced life as a store boy at Canton, in Cumberland County, Virginia, and prospered greatly as a merchant in Canton, Cumberland Court House, New Canton, and Richmond, and Oxford, North Carolina. On his second marriage, Mr. R. K. Dabney settled on his wife's land in Powhatan County, Virginia.

Colonel William Pope, the father of Mrs. Robert K. Dabney, was descended from Nathaniel Pope, the first settler, whose daughter married Colonel John Washington, father of Lawrence, father of Augustine, who was father of George Washington, who was born at the paternal mansion at Pope's Creek, Westmoreland County, Virginia. General John Pope, of the United States army is a descendant from this same Nathaniel Pope.

RECORD NO. 128

(Furnished by Judge William Pope Dabney.)

Judge William Pope Dabney, son of Robert Kelso Dabney and Lucy Ann Pope, and his wife, Miss Lula Madison.

SIXTH GENERATION.

First.—Robert Kelso is an enterprising railroad builder in Texas.

Second.—Percy Pope has just graduated in law at the University of Virginia.

Third.—Lula married William Marshall Taylor.

Fourth.—Julia Byrd unmarried.

Fifth.—William Champe.

Sixth.—James Madison.

OBSERVATIONS.

Judge Dabney was named for his maternal grandfather. He married Miss Lula Madison, a grand niece of President Madison, and served in the Virginia Legislature, and all through the Civil War. In 1872 he was elected Judge of the County Court of Powhatan and Cumberland, and remained in office until Mahone came into power, and after his overthrow, he was again elected in 1855–6, by the Legislature of that year, which office he still holds at date (1887).

Mrs. Dabney was the daughter of Colonel Ambrose Madison, of Orange, Virginia, son of General William Madison, who was a brother of President James Madison. General Madison was Lieutenant of Artillery at the siege of Yorktown, and Brigadier-General in the war of 1812, and was at Yorktown in "Dabney's Legion."

Judge William Pope Dabney states: "My father, Robert Kelso Dabney, had only two children—myself and brother Robert. We were both educated at Hampden Sydney College, and the University of Virginia; and when the war commenced we were both large landowners and slaveholders, and both had served in the Virginia Legislature. Both of us volunteered as Confederate Soldiers in the Fourth Virginia Cavalry, and both survived the war."

RECORD NO. 129
(Given by Judge William Pope Dabney.)

Robert Dabney, second son of Robert Kelso Dabney, and Lucy Ann Pope, and his wife, Miss Nannie Marye.

SIXTH GENERATION.

First.—John L.

Second.—Marye D.

Third.—Lucy Kelso.

Fourth.—William Pope; dead.

Fifth.—Evelyn.

Sixth.—Nannie Cary Selden, of Duluth.

Seventh.—Robert.

OBSERVATIONS.

Mr. Robert Dabney was a graduate of Hampden Sydney College, and the University of Virginia, and was an L. L. D. of William and Mary College. When the Civil War commenced he volunteered as a Confederate Soldier, and served through the war. By emancipation he became utterly ruined, but being an accomplished scholar and a friend of Dr. William H. McGaffey, of the University of Virginia, through him he obtained a Professorship of Mental Philosophy, Logic, and English Literature, at the University of the South, at Sewanee, Tennessee, where he died in 1876, much lamented. His pupils erected a monument to his memory in the University Grounds. His wife was born on Marye's Heights. One of her brothers was Lieutenant-Governor, and another is the present Auditor of State. Mrs. Dabney died in the winter of 1886-7.

RECORD NO. 130
(Supplied by Cornelius J. M. Dabney, of Selma, Arkansas.)

* Cornelius Dabney, father of Simpson Harrison Dabney, of Arkansas, son of————, and————, and his wife.

* Probably Cornelius, son of John Dabney, of Spottsylvania. (See Waller Record.)

SUPPOSED FIFTH GENERATION.

First.—John.

Second.—Robert.

Third.—Simpson Harrison, father of Cornelius J. M. Dabney, of Selma, Arkansas.

Fourth.—A daughter.

Fifth.—A daughter.

Sixth.—A daughter.

Seventh.—A daughter.

OBSERVATIONS.

Cornelius J. M. Dabney, of Selma, Drew County, Arkansas, writes: "All the old people are dead, and I can give but little information. Our family came from Virginia to Maury County, Tennessee, and from thence to Louisiana, and then to Arkansas. My father, two brothers and four sisters, came to this country. I was named for my grandfather. I have only one brother, and he lives in Tulare City, California. His name is N. H. Dabney. I have three sisters, all married. My father has been dead sixteen years. He was the youngest son of Cornelius Dabney, and he was born in 1811. (This would make him to have been sixty years of age at his death.) We are of French descent, and descended from the Virginia family you speak of."

RECORD NO. 131

(Supplied by Enoch B. Dabney and I. T. Dabney.)

Father of Nathan and William Dabney (name unknown.) He had three sons and several daughters. Only the two above named are known, viz.:

SEVENTH GENERATION.

First.—William married, and had several sons.

Second.—Nathan married Jane Younger in 1790, in Virginia.

OBSERVATIONS.

Enoch B. Dabney, of La Plata, Missouri, writes: "My great grandfather, Nathan Dabney, was a native of Virginia, near

Lynchburg. He always claimed that his grandfather and a brother came to Virginia from Turkey (?) and that they were the only two Dabneys who came to this country, and settled in Virginia. Nathan's parents died when he was small. One of his brothers was named William, and had several sons."

Mr. Enoch B. Dabney has been a generous assistant in this work since the death of the author by adding largely to his subscription of books, and advancing money to aid in the publication.

F. D.

RECORD NO. 132

(Given by E. B. Dabney, of La Plata, Missouri).

Record of William Dabney, brother of Nathan Dabney. He had five sons, viz.:

FOURTH GENERATION.

First.—Benjamin lived in Southern Kentucky.

Second.—George lived in Southern Kentucky.

Third.—Charles moved to Eastern Tennessee.

Fourth.—John lived in Southern Kentucky.

Fifth.—William lived in Shelby County, Kentucky.

OBSERVATIONS.

It is supposed that William Dabney accompanied his brother Nathan from Virginia, near Lynchburg, in 1808. He lived awhile in Wayne County, Kentucky, and afterwards moved to Indiana. His son, Benjamin, when only fourteen years of age, went into the army during the war of Revolution, and was at the Battle of Guilford Court House.

RECORD NO. 133

(Given by E. B. Dabney and I. T. Dabney.)

Nathan Dabney, son of————, and—————, and his wife, Jane Younger. They had five sons and five daughters, viz.:

FIFTH GENERATION.

First.—Sophia, born in Virginia, January 20, 1791.

Second.—Pamelia, born in Virginia, May 23, 1793.

Third.—Jubal, born in Virginia, July 25, 1795; married Mary Sheeks.

Fourth.—Rhoda, born in Virginia, June 23, 1797.

Fifth.—Bluford, born in Virginia, August 21, 1799; married Rebecca Vickery.

Sixth.—Elizabeth, born in Virginia, October 7, 1801.

Seventh.—Tyree, born in Virginia, August 5, 1803; married Irene Ellis.

Eighth.—Jane, born in Virginia, October 2, 1805.

Ninth.—Nathan, Jr., born in Virginia, February 29, 1808; married Kaziah Ellis in 1834. Died in 1877, and his wife soon after.

Tenth.—Thomas Jefferson, born in Wayne County, Kentucky, July 27, 1810; married Cassanna Walker in 1837. They were the second couple married in that County. Both are living near Millard, Adair County, Missouri, at date (1887).

OBSERVATIONS.

Nathan Dabney, Sr., moved from Virginia to Cumberland County, Kentucky, in 1808, and in 1833, he moved again to Macon County, Missouri, where he died. He was one of the pioneer settlers of Macon County, and was the first County Assessor.

Thomas Jefferson Dabney was also a pioneer settler in Macon County, and served as a member of the County Court from 1837 to 1842.

I. T. Dabney does not say which of the above sons was the father of J. B. Dabney and himself.

RECORD NO. 134
(Given by E. B. Dabney.)

Nathan Dabney, Jr., son of Nathan Dabney, Sr., and Jane Younger, and his wife, Kaziah Ellis.

SIXTH GENERATION.

First.—Melinda married Mr. Sears, of Callao, Missouri, and is living at date (1887), in that place.

M

Second.—Dr. William P. living (1887), in Powell, Arkansas.

Third.—J. W. living at Atlanta, Missouri, 1887; married Sarah H. Baity, July, 1856.

Fourth.—Ellis B. married Nancy Gilbreath. Died in Macon County, Missouri, in 1873, leaving four children, viz.: Albert, Ida, Thomas and Ellis.

RECORD NO. 135
(Given by E. B. Dabney.)

J. W. Dabney above, and his wife, Sarah H. Baity.

SIXTH GENERATION.

First.—Enoch B., born 1857; married Sarah E. Soddrel, 1882; living at date in La Plata, Missouri, and has three children—Beulah, born 1882; Edith, born 1884, and Grover Cleveland, born 1887.

Second.—Charles W.

Third.—John W.

Fourth.—Goodson.

Fifth.—Sidney.

OBSERVATIONS.

I. T. Dabney, of Savannah, Davis County, Iowa, and brother to J. B. Dabney, of Iowa, in a letter dated July 22d, 1884, says: "I can go no farther back than when my ancestor came to the United States from Turkey. He was a Turk (?) and my great grandfather. He had three sons and some daughters. Their names I do not know, excepting my grandfather, whose name was Nathan. One of them, my great uncle, had some sons. Their names were: Benjamin, George, Charles, John and William. Charles went to East Tennessee. George, John and Benjamin lived in South Kentucky, and William in Shelby, Kentucky. My grandfather, uncle to the above named boys, moved to Kentucky from Virginia in 1808. He had five sons and five daughters. The boys' names were: Jubal, Bluford, Tyree, Nathan and Jefferson. I can give you the names of their sons if you wish."

I. T. Dabney states: "My grandfather, Nathan, moved to Kentucky in 1808. The father of the above named sons must have moved also to Kentucky, as nearly all his sons appear to have resided in that State."

Dr. W. P. Dabney, of Powell, Arkansas, says: "My great grandfather was from France, but claimed to be of Turkish origin. My grandfather was a native of Virginia, and was a soldier in the Revolutionary War. His name was Nathan. He moved to Kentucky in the early part of 1800; then to St. Louis, Missouri, and died in Macon County, Missouri, about the year 1848. My father was born near Lynchburg, Virginia, in the year 1794. He was raised in Wayne County, Kentucky, moved to Missouri in 1820, and died in Macon County, Missouri, in 1871. He had four brothers older than himself, and his mother was a Younger. C. C. Dabney, of Lewisburg, Tennessee, can probably give you some more information on this subject. I think, from what information I have heard, that all the Dabneys are offshoots from the first family of that name that came over, and they are generally professional men. All my relations have black hair, dark complexions, and are tall, and live to be old. They make plenty of money, and spend it the same way."

Enoch B. Dabney, of La Plata, Missouri, says: "My father lives ten miles from here, out of town. All the Dabneys whom I have ever met are directly related to me. My great grandfather was from Virginia; was named Nathan or Nathaniel, and was of Turkish descent (?)"

Dr. Charles William Dabney, Jr., President of the University of Tennessee, says: "I think that Dr. W. P. Dabney, of Powell, Arkansas, is a descendant from the Dabneys, of Lynchburg, Virginia."

Not one of the above say who their father was, but only name their grandfather, Nathan.

RECORD NO. 136

Mrs. Malinda Sears, of Callao, Missouri, in a letter forwarded after Mr. Dabney's sudden death, writes: " I think my grandfather, Nathan Dabney, had a brother George, and another named Benjamin." She further says: " That Nathan's brother Benjamin (not William, as Mr. Dabney has it), was father of the five boys, Benjamin, George, Charles, John and William. She also states that Tyree, son of Nathan, was father of her cousins, I. T. and J. B. Dabney, of Savannah, Iowa."

Mrs. Sears' father was Nathan 2d, who married Keziah Ellis, and had ten children, of whom only three are now living (1887), viz: J. W. Dabney, of Atlanta, Missouri; Dr. W. P. Dabney, of Powell, Arkansas, and herself. Mrs. Sears was married first, to W. C. Bernard, moved to Texas, and had three children—E. E. Bernard, of Saratoga, Wyoming Territory, Alberina Ashley, of Fort Steele, Wyoming Territory, and H. C. Bernard, of Laramie City, Wyoming Territory. After Mr. Bernard's death, his wife returned to Missouri, married Martin Sears, and has two children, Effie M. and Albert M. Sears.

Another item in Mrs. Sears' letter explains why this branch of the family claim to be of Turkish orgin. She says of her grandfather Nathan, " His *mother* was of Turkish descent." A simple solution of a mystery that had baffled research for two years.

RECORD NO. 137

Cornelius Dabney, the father of Henry, and grandfather of Dr. F. K. Dabney, of Wano, Kansas.

First.—Henry, born in 1796, in the vicinity of Richmond, Virginia; emigrated to Vincennes, Indiana, in 1824, and afterwards to Illinois, and there married Maria Stanfield, and died March 25th, 1869, at seventy-four years of age. They were the parents of Dr. F. K. Dabney.

Second.—Robert, who, if living, resides in Versailles, Woodford County, Kentucky.

OBSERVATIONS.

Dr. F. K. Dabney, of Wano, Kansas, states: " My father's name was Henry. He was born and raised in the vicinity of Richmond, Virginia. Grandfather's name was Cornelius, I think. Father was born in 1796, and served three campaigns in the war of 1812. About 1824 he emigrated to Vincennes, Indiana, where he was Principal of a school for some years. He afterwards moved to Illinois, where he married Miss Maria Stanfield. There were born to them nine sons and three daughters, all but one yet living. Father died March 25th, 1869, at seventy-three years of age. Mother is living (1887); nearly eighty years of age."

Mr. J. Peale Dabney, of Salem, Massachusetts, who is a descendant of Robert and Elizabeth d'Aubigné, and who was an ardent genealogist, as far as related to his family, and who died in 1868, stated to his cousin, William Dabney, of Providence, Rhode Island (and this same idea was cherished by him during his life, and by his brothers and sisters, and by them transmitted to their descendants), that "About the time that Robert and Elizabeth d'Aubigné came to Boston, two brothers of his emigrated to, and settled in Virginia."

This tradition has been abundantly confirmed by the same tradition as regards Robert d'Aubigné being related to them, which is universally entertained among the scattered members of the Virginia Dabneys, who are the descendants of John and Cornelius d'Aubigné, as we have already seen in the foregoing.

INDEX TO THE DABNEY RECORDS—FIRST OR ELDER BRANCH.

INDEX TO SECOND BRANCH—GEORGE DABNEY'S DESCENDANTS.

NAMES.	PARENTS.	GENERATION	RECORD No.	PAGE.
George Dabney	Cornelius d'Aubigné	3	40	94
George Dabney 2d	George Dabney 1st	4	41	94
Colonel James Dabney and Judith Anderson	George Dabney 2d	5	42	95
William Dabney and Sarah Watson	Colonel James Dabney and Judith Anderson	6	43	97
Maria Dabney and Colonel Samuel Carr	William Dabney and Sarah Watson	6	44	99
Mary Senora Dabney and William B. M. Perkins	William Dabney and Sarah Watson	6	45	99
Walter Davies Dabney and Miss Sappington	William Dabney and Sarah Watson	6	46	99
William Dabney and Susan Fitzhugh Greene, nee Gordon	William Dabney and Sarah Watson			
Sarah Dabney and William Winston	William Dabney and Sarah Watson	6	47	100
William Dabney, of Aldringham, and Miss Barrett	George Dabney 1st	4	48	101
Captain George Dabney and Elizabeth Price	George Dabney 1st	4	49	101
William Dabney and Mehetable Hylton	William Dabney and Miss Barrett	5	50	103
Martha Dabney and Jefferson Stuart	Captain George Dabney and Elizabeth Price	6	51	106
Nancy Dabney and Judge Alexander Stuart	William Dabney and Mehetable Hylton	6	52	106
Archibald Stuart and Elizabeth Pannell	Captain George Dabney and Elizabeth Price	5	53	107
John Dabney and Susanna D. Morris	Judge Alexander Stuart and Nancy Dabney	6	54	107
John Blair Dabney and Elizabeth Lewis Towles	Captain George Dabney and Elizabeth Price	5	55	108
John Dabney and Lavinia Langhorne	John Dabney and Susanna Morris	7	56	109
Maria Louisa Dabney and William C. Carrington	John Blair Dabney and Elizabeth L. Towles	8	57	113
Susan Morris Dabney and Edmund Taylor	John Blair Dabney and Elizabeth L. Towles	8	58	114
Kelle Lewis Dabney and Peter Saunders	John Blair Dabney and Elizabeth L. Towles	8	59	114
Chiswell Dabney and Lucy Dabney Fontaine	John Blair Dabney and Elizabeth L. Towles	8	60	115
Elizabeth Dabney and Lynn Shackleford	John Blair Dabney and Elizabeth L. Towles	8	61	115
Chiswell Dabney and Miss Norvell	Captain George Dabney and Miss Price	5	62	116
Elizabeth Dabney and John S. Langhorne	Captain George Dabney and Miss Price	5	63	116
Samuel Dabney and Miss Merriwether	Chiswell Dabney and Miss Norvell	7	64	118
	William Dabney, of Aldringham, and Miss Barrett	5	66	123

INDEX TO SECOND BRANCH—GEORGE DABNEY'S DESCENDANTS.—CONTINUED.

INDEX TO THIRD BRANCH—CORNELIUS AND SARAH JENNINGS DABNEY'S DESCENDANTS.

INDEX TO THIRD BRANCH—CORNELIUS AND SARAH JENNINGS DABNEY'S DESCENDANTS.—Continued.

ERRATA.

In Records 40, 41, 42 and 43, Mr. Dabney has followed his usual form, and given the generation of the children, while Records 44, 45, 46 and 47 give the generation of the parents, a change of form which was not observed until too late to correct it.

In Records 53, 55, for George Dabney and Miss Barrett, read George Dabney and Elizabeth Price.

Record 111, read fourth generation.

A discrepancy occurs in the Records of the First Branch of the Dabneys, which I am not able to reconcile.

In Record No. 7, supplied by the late Thomas S. Dabney, Benjamin Dabney married Miss Armistead, and (Record 8) was father of—first, George, married to Susan Littlepage Quarles; second, Benjamin, married his cousin, Ann West Dabney.

N. B.—Ann West Dabney, ighter of George Dabney and Miss Quarles would, in this case, be niece, not cousin of Benjamin.

In Record No. 9, supplied by Mrs. Robinson, George Dabney, who married Miss Quarles, was son of George Dabney, of Dabney's Ferry, which, as both Mr. Dabney and Mrs. Robinson agree in stating that Benjamin and Ann West Dabney were cousins, would seem to be correct.

Again, in Records 9 and 10, Mrs. Robinson says Benjamin, who married Ann West Dabney, was son of Benjamin and Miss Armistead; and in Record 10, that Ann West Dabney was the oldest child of George Dabney, of Dabney's Ferry, and Miss Quarles.

This last statement conflicts with Record No. 9, which says she was his grand-daughter.